Garden Design

A Book of Ideas

Garden Design
A Book of Ideas

Heidi Howcroft & Marianne Majerus

FIREFLY BOOKS

A FIREFLY BOOK

Published by Firefly Books Ltd. 2015

To Rob Cassy

First printing

**Publisher Cataloging-in-Publication
Data (U.S.)**

A CIP record for this title is available from
the Library of Congress

**Library and Archives Canada
Cataloguing in Publication**

A CIP record for this title is available from
Library and Archives Canada

Published in the United States by
Firefly Books (U.S.) Inc.
P.O. Box 1338, Ellicott Station
Buffalo, New York 14205

Published in Canada by
Firefly Books Ltd.
50 Staples Avenue, Unit 1
Richmond Hill, Ontario L4B 0A7

Printed and bound in China

First published in Great Britain in
2015 by Mitchell Beazley
an imprint of Octopus Publishing
Group Ltd, Endeavour House,
189 Shaftesbury Avenue, London
WC2H 8JY

For Mitchell Beazley
Publisher: Alison Starling; Senior
Editor: Leanne Bryan; Copy Editor:
Helen Ridge; Proofreader: Mandy
Greenfield; Indexer: Helen Snaith;
Executive Art Editor: Juliette
Norsworthy; Designers: Abigail
Read and Grace Helmer; Senior
Production Manager: Katherine
Hockley

CONTENTS

INTRODUCTION

Every garden, irrespective of whether it is a crate on top of a barge or parkland surrounding a country mansion, is a personal piece of paradise, tailor-made for the individual. Making a garden goes far beyond the instinct to grow food for the family and is a desire to embellish and enhance one's personal space.

Some gardens are meticulously planned, while others just happen. There are no hard-and-fast rules for their design. It is all about personal taste, so who is to judge what is good or bad? But while our imagination knows no boundaries, the garden certainly does, and appreciating where these lie is the difference between a great design and one that is run of the mill. The first step is to establish basic parameters. Much of this is common sense, recognizing that it is better to work with, rather than against, nature.

A fundamental part of a landscape architect's education is the design process, which begins with the site analysis and culminates in the finished garden. Following these same steps will help you decide whether to go it completely alone or enlist the help of a professional designer. A design is rarely immediately apparent; in most cases, deciding on one is a matter of diligently working through a list of requirements and gathering information. Method, not magic, is the key.

The starting point is devising a brief: what you want from the garden and whether it needs to be formal or informal; the desired level of maintenance; whether the whole garden or just a section is to be designed; available funds; and if the work is to be completed in stages or all at once. The size of the garden is just as important as its setting, with designs for a 'blank canvas' garden belonging to a new build and the revamp of an existing mature garden, for example, being completely different.

Before charging in with a bulldozer or pickaxe, look at your garden through the windows of the house, from the sofa or the kitchen. Observe what there is now and try to visualize what you would like to see in the future. Pinning a picture of a favourite garden to the window and looking at it and your garden simultaneously does help you decide if that style is either a 'fit' or just a romantic notion. Creating mood boards and gathering photographs of other gardens, images of garden furniture, and details of plants and paving are all a huge help in the decision-making process, as are pictures from various angles of the site itself. It is often at this point that the decision is made either to go it alone or employ an expert. When seeking advice, consult members of professional bodies, such as the Landscape Institute and the Society of Garden Designers. Beware of cowboys who promise paradise for nothing; there is always a catch.

A site survey in which topography, heights, boundaries, existing features and vegetation are shown to scale is invaluable when designing. Armed with this information, together with your brief and mood boards, preliminary sketches can be made. These can then be narrowed down to favourites and developed further into an overall design. Living with and looking at the design and fine-tuning details over a period of time pays dividends. Staking out the outline of paths and patios, even using stepladders draped with sheets to give an idea of the volume of large shrubs, are all useful tools to see if a design could work.

Like a suit, a garden has to fit, have a shape yet be comfortable. But while it is possible to try on clothes before making a commitment, it is a different matter with gardens. Garden open days are a great way of getting to know other gardens. Few people garden on a grand scale, so these domestic, private retreats are perfect for getting a feel for your likes and dislikes and deciding on a style. Taking a broad view and looking at gardens abroad or from the past can also be inspiring – it is all a matter of interpretation.

Without the marvellous work done by landscape architects, architects, garden designers and owners, as well as the gardeners who maintain the exemplary schemes, we would not have any material to show you in this book. Thank you to all of you for providing such a wealth of ideas. There is a garden out there to suit every one of us; it is merely waiting to be discovered.

BASICS

WHERE IS YOUR GARDEN?

The location of your garden is one of the most important factors when deciding on its design. Is it in a city or a town, in a village or the countryside, in a valley, up a mountain, or on the coast? Knowing and appreciating what is around you helps to determine what is possible and what is not. Making a successful garden is a challenge, and every bit of information about the surroundings, climate, soil, and what grows well locally makes for a better design.

1 Country gardens are the ultimate dream for many keen gardeners and city dwellers. Plots tend to be larger than their urban counterparts, and in mature gardens there may be well-established planting. Assessing the site – determining what is already there and recognizing the potential – is the first step towards creating a good design.

2 Hemmed in on all sides, with space at a premium, gardens in the city are highly prized. Every inch of space, whether on the ground, a flat roof, a balcony, or a raised level, is valuable and can be transformed into an urban oasis, as with the High Line in Manhattan, shown here.

3 Suburban gardens are secluded private retreats – blank canvases that can be designed in a multitude of ways. The only restrictions are personal taste and planning laws.

4 Gardens in extreme locations, as here on the coast or on the fringes of arid or highland areas, are more of a design challenge. It's not just the plants that must be capable of withstanding the extreme conditions, but also the hard-landscaping materials and any structures.

1

Architecture and Surroundings

The house and garden go hand in hand, with the one enhancing and complementing the other. Together, they should form a whole, with neither vying for attention, and the garden should be designed with this in mind.

The architecture of the house can trigger a specific garden style that picks up elements of its design. Large windows, glass screens, and folding doors create opportunities to open up views to the garden. More time is often spent looking out at the garden from the house than actually being in it, so pay attention to what can be seen from the inside. Building materials for the house could also be used in the garden for walls, fencing, even paving, creating a unity that is particularly important for small gardens.

1 Views work both ways. This townhouse is screened by a mature tree enveloped in wisteria, giving the impression of a much leafier location. The view from the windows is of a lush green town square.

2 Unsightly walls, so often the bane of urban areas, can be disguised and enhanced. The French are past masters in the use of trellises to clad walls and they have also introduced the concept of vertical green façades. Inspired by epiphytes growing on trees in the tropics, a system has been developed whereby plants such as perennials and ferns grow on matting held in frames. Starter kits are available for domestic use, as shown in this example in San Francisco.

3 Outbuildings can be inspiring. Who would have thought this was once a pigsty? The bog garden in front, filled with primulas and ferns, is an ideal use of the churned-up ground and in keeping with the atmosphere of the setting.

4 Looking beyond boundaries and recognizing the potential of the surroundings is important when designing a garden. The adjoining fields have been cleverly incorporated into this garden designed by Chris Ghyselen, who has "borrowed" the landscape in order to enhance the view. Similarly, in a suburban garden, a neighbour's tree could form a valuable backdrop.

Why Does the Weather Matter?

Climatic conditions determine what grows well in our gardens and also how we use them. Each region of the earth has a specific palette of plants and materials that defines its character. This gives gardens their individual look, making a garden in the Arizona desert, for example, quite different from one in subtropical Brazil or the heart of the English countryside. While there is always the temptation to push boundaries when it comes to planting, there is a limit to what can be grown. Adapting to and accepting climatic conditions makes for healthier gardens and should not stifle design.

1 Few of us think in terms of global weather patterns. We are more concerned with local matters: the prevailing wind, frost, snow, rainfall, hours of sunshine, and temperature. Here, the early morning sun warms up the soil, highlighting the prairie planting, which thrives in continental climates of hot summers and cold winters.

2 While frost has a certain beauty, it does limit the range of plants that will survive. The 19th-century notion that plants can acclimatize has long been abandoned and it is accepted that plants do best in situations that match their natural habitat. Winter hardiness zones ranging from coldest to warmest are an essential guide when selecting plants.

3 Hedges and pleached avenues are useful wind barriers, filtering the force of the wind to create sheltered gardens. Moisture-laden mist makes for an eerie atmosphere, reducing the shapes of the trees to silhouettes. Mist and dew are valuable sources of moisture, which many plants rely on for growth.

4 The amount of rainfall determines to a great extent which plants will flourish. Most garden owners yearn for gentle rain, preferably at night, but the reality is often different. With weather patterns becoming increasingly unpredictable, the ability to harvest rainwater should be an integral part of garden design. Similarly, the choice of plants and materials needs to suit the environment, as shown here in the gardens of Sleightholmedale, North Yorkshire.

Knowing Your Soil

Soil is more than a surface covering. It is also a reflection of the geology beneath the surface, which lends identity to a place and determines the vegetation that grows there naturally.

Good gardens have healthy plants that flourish because they are suited to the soil. Soils are classified according to type, particle size, and pH (the measure of acidity). Few people, other than the most avid gardeners, select their house based on soil type. Existing vegetation is a pretty good indication of what will grow in the area, so it pays to walk around a new neighbourhood to see what is flourishing. Removing and replacing existing soil is a costly and messy operation and can result in a plant mix that might please the owner but does not fit into the surroundings and, therefore, is not ecologically sound.

1 Boggy waterlogged soils can be drained, but there is a range of plants that flourish naturally in such conditions. Trees such as alder, willow, and swamp cypress, and water's-edge plants like iris, *Eupatorium cannabinum*, and *Lythrum salicaria*, are cases in point.

2 The thin, calcareous (chalky) soils found in the Alps or on the English Dorset coast, as shown here (see also pages 206–7), are characterized by sparse tree cover and extensive wild-flower meadows. However, in gardens where the soil has been worked and enhanced, different vegetation is possible.

3 A causeway between two ponds leads to a deciduous woodland. The soil is dark and rich and prone to flooding, which spreads a fine silt over the surface. Sycamore, horse chestnut, and birch are some of the trees that can tolerate short periods of flooding.

4 Friable garden soil enriched with organic matter before planting provides an excellent growing medium, with good moisture retention and plant nutrients. Heavy clay soils composed of fine particles can be improved by working in organic matter, to open and loosen the soil.

5 Gorse and heather are both indicators of acidic soil. Here, the situation is exacerbated by the steep slope and the exposure to erosion. In such situations, only the strongest plants will survive, with their roots forming a "mat" that binds and retains the soil.

What Do You Want from Your Garden?

A core element of garden design is function. Knowing how and when the garden will be used shapes its design.

The days of gardens existing solely to provide food for the table are long gone, although there is renewed interest in growing vegetables. Today, gardens fulfil a greater, often multifaceted role. More than being just decorative green spaces, they are where we live, play, entertain, relax, or reconnect with nature. They can inspire and be a retreat or a work of art in themselves. No matter whether a garden is large or small, it should be tailored to the lifestyle of the user.

1 Leisure and entertaining are concentrated in one area in this small London garden designed by Spencer Viner (see also pages 32–3). The hammock is for relaxing but when it's taken down, the space opens out and becomes somewhere to get together with friends.

2 Nature lovers would feel at home in this relaxed country garden set in an orchard. Gardens are not made just for enjoyment; they have an important role as an eco-niche for flora and fauna. Encouraging birds and bees has become even more important, given their dwindling numbers.

3 Gardens can be a showcase, a place for plant collections, or a wonderful scene that can be admired from inside in all seasons, as in this garden by Sam Martin.

4 How we use our gardens changes as we grow older. For families with young children, the garden is a private playground, where children can explore, play ball games, or build sandcastles in the sandpit, as in this San Francisco garden by Arterra Landscape Architects.

5 Come the first rays of sunshine, out come the T-shirts and the barbecues. Outdoor cooking has never been so popular, with dedicated equipment demanding a special place in the garden, as provided here by Declan Buckley.

The Importance of Time

Plants need time to grow, a garden needs time to mature, and we need time to look after it and also enjoy it. Evaluating honestly how many spare hours are available for maintaining the garden can help to decide on the right design. For example, if weeding is not your idea of fun, think before planting an extensive flower border. All gardens need more attention in the initial years, so if a lot of thought and money have been spent to create the ideal scheme but your own time is in short supply, go that extra mile and employ someone to help you.

Instant gardens are an option for impatient owners with large budgets, but part of the joy of having a garden is nurturing it and watching it grow and take shape. Learning its foibles, fine-tuning and tinkering, is all part of the experience, as is discovering whether the plants that you grow perform in the same way as those described in books or on the Internet.

Making a garden is not something we can repeat every year, nor is it a quick fix. It is there for the duration, developing and maturing as we do. Many gardens outlast their makers and are unique legacies, enjoyed by generations to come.

Many plants, like the maidenhair tree (*Ginkgo biloba*), are links with the past, reaching as far back in time as the dinosaurs. Tree ferns (*Dicksonia antarctica*) measuring 2m (6½ft) in height are aged gentlemen of the plant world, 200 years old or more, while majestic oaks, limes, and California redwoods are true ancients. Gardening is part of our primeval self – the instinct to grow and cultivate is as strong today as it was in the past.

1 Ideally, there should be a space in the garden for every distinct time of day, as in this roof garden designed by Amir Schlezinger: somewhere to enjoy breakfast in the sunshine and al fresco summer lunches in the shade, a sheltered spot to make the most of the winter sun, and an uninterrupted view to soak up the sunset. Being able to observe how the sun moves around the garden throughout the year, to see where shadows are cast and for how long, can only enrich a design.

Working with the Seasons

A garden is a living calendar, marking out the progression of the year. Winter is monochrome, with sharpened silhouettes. Spring, meanwhile, is full of yellow and lime-greens, and all shades in between. As spring rolls into summer, blues and reds appear, followed by a full palette of colours, often in astonishing combinations. Autumn is the time for russets, oranges, and reds, making a final flourish before the temperature drops and the days shorten. Paying heed to these characteristics is sure to add variety and highlights to a garden and produce dynamic designs.

1 Views and volume change with the seasons, as do light and shade. Framed by hornbeam hedges in full leaf, this restricted view is channelled towards the bottom pool, enveloped by dense vegetation.

2 The same garden, designed by Marc Schoellen, appears larger in winter as the views open up. The contours of the water basin are visible, as are the dark shades of the pool at the foot of the main axis.

3 Even though these hedges are still relatively young, their deep matt green colour makes them appear quite mature. With the mass of burgeoning green shapes in the summer garden, it is difficult to determine what lies in the distance.

4 The highlight of the gardening year for this flower garden is summer, when shrubs and perennials seem to vie for attention, adding layer after layer of interest.

5 The bare bones of the design (3) and the youthful delicacy of the planting are even more apparent in winter, when views into the distance are opened up and the garden appears less enclosed. The russet leaves of the hornbeam hedge add colour to an otherwise monochrome time of year.

6 In the past, when country houses were used as a summer residence, and owners retreated to the towns for the rest of the year, little attention was paid to how a garden looked in winter. This has changed. Gardens like those at Gravetye Manor, West Sussex, shown here in winter and above (4) in summer, are now on display all year round. Seed heads, ornamental grasses, and semi-evergreen shrubs take on an added beauty when dusted by hoar frost.

A QUESTION OF STYLE

DESIGNS FOR ALL TASTES

How a garden is designed is entirely up to the owner. There is no right or wrong style, just personal choice, but the range of styles – historical, contemporary, country, cottage, naturalistic – can be daunting. The only constraints, which should be checked during the design phase, involve structures requiring planning permission, such as fences and how high they can be, and limits on the use of impermeable surfaces. Visit as many gardens as possible for inspiration.

1 Clarity in design helps to knit the old and the new together. In this garden, which has been designed by Sara Jane Rothwell, the boundary and the retaining walls have been painted white, giving a contemporary edge to the park-like garden beyond.

2 Existing trees can provide the impetus for a garden style. The arched branches of an old cherry tree provide the frame for this Japanese-inspired garden by Sam Martin. Strategically positioning selected elements, such as the maple and the bamboo waterspout, introduces a feeling of tranquillity to the space.

3 Vegetables can form the focus of a garden, combining function with aesthetics, as in this kitchen garden by Julie Toll (see also pages 50–1).

4 Recognizing the potential of mature gardens, then reshaping and invigorating them, is one of the trickiest tasks for a designer. Bold, dramatic designs take courage but they can work exceptionally well, breathing new life into the garden, as François Valentiny demonstrates here.

1

CASE STUDY
New Country

South of Dublin, on the edges of the Wicklow Mountains, new gardens are being created that are redefining the image of a country garden. Quirky and individual, but rooted in Ireland's rich gardening heritage, these gardens are showing the way forward. They celebrate gardening and the joy of collecting and growing unusual plants, yet seek inspiration from the landscape.

In among them is June Blake's garden and nursery, which have gradually evolved over the past 15 years. As her confidence has grown, so have her ideas. From humble beginnings, the garden and field around the estate manager's house have been transformed. The dense stand of trees that once encroached on the building was thinned, and a central flower garden, arranged over four generously proportioned beds, was created as a showcase for plants from the nursery, while areas of semi-shade were added to the fringes of the garden.

1 The sloping pasture above the central flowerbeds is the most recent addition to the 1.2-hectare (3-acre) garden, creating a natural transition to the surrounding countryside. A broad, mown path, punctuated by timber ribs, leads to a lookout platform (top left) subtly worked into the hillside.

2 Formal and informal meet in the heart of the garden. A box hedge threads its way through the flowerbed, dividing and joining the exuberant cottage-style planting of geranium, dierama, camassia, allium, eryngium, and more, in a master-class of plant design.

3 Contrasting textures and harmonizing tones are an important aspect of this garden. The calm, shallow, reflective pool, edged with Cor-Ten™ steel and surrounded by a pebble border in a narrow frame of old stone setts, is like a picture superimposed on the gravel path. Old and new, traditional and contemporary, are recurring themes in this garden. The vernacular architecture of the dry-stone retaining wall works surprisingly well with the recently built concrete retaining wall.

CASE STUDY

International Chic Minimalism

Ever since André le Nôtre set the tone of garden design with Versailles in the 17th century, there has been a fascination with formal design. Modern interpretations have taken the essential elements and cleverly reconfigured them, to create contemporary, clean, and elegant gardens, which are equally at home in London, Paris, Milan, Berlin, or New York – in fact, any place where hornbeam, box, yew, and a manicured lawn grow well.

The landscape architectural practice of del Buono Gazerwitz has honed the design of contemporary, lush, minimalist gardens to a fine art. Recognizing the importance of scale, their gardens are not swamped with vegetation and artefacts, but celebrated as calm, open spaces and opportunities to take breath. Boundaries are layered and cleverly camouflaged by hedges. Using a palette of geometric shapes – plants clipped into cubes and spheres – set off by lawns and linear, light-coloured paths, the practice has put its mark on a number of urban gardens, primarily in London.

1 Size and scale are vital in garden design, especially in town gardens hemmed in on all sides. The success of this scheme, which is appreciated as much through the windows of the house as from within the garden, lies in its beguiling simplicity. Amelanchiers, with extra-high stems and airy canopies, flank the hornbeam hedge. Low blocks of box (*Buxus sempervirens*) add a formal note. Every single component here has been very carefully considered.

2 Spacious gardens can accommodate larger shrubs and trees. Pleached hornbeam with slender trunks set in front of the boundary, together with a row of oversized box balls, lead the eye onwards, towards the steps and patio, accentuating the garden's length.

3 Framed by clipped box and yew hedging, the open lawn appears larger and more generously proportioned than it really is. By deliberately reducing the colour palette to green and white, emphasis is placed on the architectural quality of the planting.

CASE STUDY
Small Is Beautiful

With real-estate costs so high in all the major cities, even the tiniest outdoor urban space is worth transforming into a personal paradise.

Garden designer Spencer Viner's small London garden demonstrates that its success has nothing to do with size or money but is all down to the imaginative use of plants, materials, and colours.

This vibrant, lush space belies the maxim that large trees have no place in a small garden. Lime trees (*Tilia cordata*), an Indian bean tree (*Catalpa bignonioides*), and even a weeping willow (*Salix babylonica*) have all been shoehorned in. The secret to their success is hard pruning and restricting the roots so that, like bonsai, the trees cannot develop to their full size.

1 Unusual combinations of materials define this garden, from the metal tubular struts of the pergola over the seating area to the glass resting on the bleached grey Spanish oak table top. Shapes and colours also play an important role. The painted yellow backdrop brings light and warmth into the space, as does the pillar-box red wall to the left.

2 A good deal of thought has been given to the choice of vegetation, which frames, highlights, and divides the garden. Clematis, wisteria, and *Trachelospermum jasminoides* (far left) are just three of the climbers that clamber up the trellis. The eclectic mix of paving material also works extremely well here, with each type delineating a different zone or mood, such as the timber decking around the weeping willow and under the bench in a tranquil corner of the garden.

3 The inventive planting pulls this garden together, from the bold foliage such as *Echium*, on the right, to the contrasting wispy grasses in their different shades of green, with the occasional flower adding height and colour. The garden is full of clever ideas like the concrete manhole rings used as plant containers and placed strategically around the garden. The ring shown here has been planted with golden *Carex elata* 'Aurea' and black-stemmed bamboo, *Phyllostachys nigra*.

City Gardens

While private gardens in many cities are usually hidden from view, London leads the way in showcasing the talents of landscape architects, designers, and green-fingered owners during garden open days. Run for charity, these are an excellent way of discovering and appreciating an astonishing range of styles that could be applied to all types of inner-city gardens.

1 Lush planting is not an option for all city gardens but, where there is sufficient light and the expectation that plants will grow well and be cared for, exuberant planting like this is possible. The natural, loose look belies the expertise required in selecting the right species in the right balance so that the planting looks good, even when not in flower. For more on this garden by Declan Buckley, see pages 232–3.

2 Striking the right balance between formality and informality is tricky. By placing *Prunus lusitanica* among the mounds of box, garden designer Charlotte Rowe has broken the rigidity of the planting. Similarly, the glowing yellow canopy of the specimen ash tree (*Fraxinus angustifolia* 'Raywood') lends an informality and lightness.

3 A garden does not have to be green; there are many examples of paved courtyards in the Arab world, where the beauty lies in patterns and textures and a single water feature. Stuart Craine has made a jacuzzi the centrepiece of his design. The textural quality of the wall is particularly appealing against the smooth paving and frothy water surface.

4 Accommodating different elements in a garden while maintaining design integrity is a juggling act: too many, and the garden is overloaded; too few, and it feels sparse. By restricting the number of materials used here, Charlotte Rowe has created a sense of harmony. Both the fence and the bench are made of the same material, while the paving slabs and gravel have the same tonal quality, all serving to draw the design together.

1

3

2

A Classic Modern Suburban Garden

The suburbs are as popular now to live in as they were at the end of the 19th century, when many were first laid out. Gardens here are generally larger than in the centre of town and often benefit from mature trees planted by previous owners.

A new owner, an extension, or general refurbishment can provide the impetus for redesigning a garden and giving it a more contemporary feel. Designs need not be dramatic, merely fitting, as in this 650-sq m (770-sq yard) suburban garden designed by Charlotte Rowe. There is a classic, modern, understated elegance and generosity about the space, which will be as fresh in 20 years' time as it is now.

1 Houses often sit proud of the garden, especially if they have a cellar or a basement. The problem is how to resolve the height difference between the reception and seating areas and the garden. Should the earth be banked up to form a slope, held back by a retaining wall, or staggered, as here? By designing three tiers, each fronted by a hedge – yew on the top two layers and box at the bottom – a problem area has been turned into a feature that looks attractive from all angles.

2 This design proves that a terrace need not be just an expanse of paving. The formality of the narrow beds is diluted by the rosemary bushes, which take on shapes of their own and fill the gaps between the regimental rows of box balls. The beds, like the water feature, link the upper and lower gardens.

3 Like a standing stone, this 1.8-m (6-ft) tall granite water feature has a Neolithic quality to it. Framed by the trunks of the pleached hornbeam and flanked by box hedges, it forms a focal point in the axis of the water channel that flows from the patio. Pleached hedges, in which nursery-trained trees with clear stems and box-shaped canopies are planted in a row to form a type of hedge on stilts, are an increasingly popular design feature. Layering has been used here to great effect, giving a sense of depth.

CASE STUDY
Grand Gestures

Much is made of grand designs in modern architecture, but there is less mention of grand, cutting-edge landscapes. The landscape architect Tom Stuart-Smith works with plants and spaces, hard landscape, and levels, to produce gardens of character that ooze a seductive beauty.

Large gardens can be daunting simply because of their size. Choosing the best design for the site and function from the wealth of possibilities on offer is a challenge. The Bauhaus maxim of less is more is a useful guide – here, it has been used to create a garden of subtle, warm colours and shapes.

1 Some gardens lend themselves to geometric shapes, others to more free-flowing forms. The secret is to soften the overriding form with contrasting elements. Here, the lines of Cor-Ten™ weathered steel edging, which step the lawn in gentle terraces, are softened by the feathery vertical thrust of the ornamental grasses and the domed box, scattered like full stops over the lawn and in the beds.

2 By using only four plant species, an exciting effect has been achieved. Variety comes from the contrasting shapes and sizes and the seasonal changes in colour. Stag's horn sumach (*Rhus typhina*), a favourite plant of the 1970s, is making a comeback. Although the suckering roots of this small, multi-stemmed tree are still a disadvantage, its umbrella-like canopy and autumn colour are hard to beat. *Hakonechloa macra*, an ornamental ground cover grass, contrasts well with the box and the russet bands of *Miscanthus* 'Purpurascens'.

3 Subtle changes in textures and tones flow through the garden, as with the feathery plumes of *Miscanthus sinensis* 'Ferner Osten', in front of the large flowerheads of *Eupatorium maculatum* (Atropurpureum Group) 'Riesenschirm'.

4 From sculptural box plants resembling haystacks and the textural brick garden wall to the reflection in the swimming pool and the sculptural "leaf" seat, each component has been carefully placed to produce a garden that is also a work of art.

LOOKING TO THE PAST

Historic landscapes and gardens are a wonderful source of inspiration. From medieval cloister gardens to Italian Renaissance gardens, from grand gardens of the French baroque to naturalistic English landscape gardens, from cottage gardens to formal rose gardens of the early 20th century, there is a wealth of styles to refer to. Visiting and experiencing as many of these as you can will help you to decide on a style that is best suited to you and your own garden.

1 Essential components of baroque gardens, vistas and hedges also have a place in contemporary gardens, as shown in this design by Tom Stuart-Smith. Parallel hedges positioned at right angles not only form a strong axis, which automatically leads the eye to the distant view, but also suggest secret, hidden spaces to the sides.

2 Using a few chosen components in a certain configuration can create a particular style. Here, classical statuary in the foreground and a clipped formal hedge behind, opening to the "wilderness" beyond, evoke the spirit of a Picturesque landscape garden.

3 Not all historic styles require acres of land. Knot gardens, in which low hedging such as box and cotton lavender (*Santolina*) are planted in overlapping patterns, can be created in the smallest space, as George Carter has done here.

4 Some historic landscapes have a surprisingly contemporary feel. This water channel at Rousham, Oxfordshire, was designed by William Kent in the 18th century.

5 Formality and geometry are the marks of a Renaissance garden, as shown in this design by George Carter.

CASE STUDY
Classical Elegance

Formal gardens convey a timeless elegance. As in stage design, nothing is left to chance: all the components are deliberately selected and placed to exude a sense of symmetry and order. Baroque gardens like Versailles are a point of reference. Vistas and paths are long and impressive, lined by hornbeam, beech, or yew hedges, cut to shape. Colours are restrained, flowers are few, and box hedges, trellises, planters, and urns decorate and enhance. Formal gardens produce an instant effect and can, if the budget allows, be planted with large plants and pre-grown hedges.

1 The hornbeam hedge encloses the space and also serves as a backdrop in this formal country garden that would suit an urban situation just as well. All the components, from the yew pyramid and elegant bench to the box parterre and box balls in planters, complement one another. Colours are restrained and coordinated, underpinning the elegance of George Carter's design.

2 Hip-high hedges of box flank the house and the central grass area in this simple design by André Van Wassenhove (see also pages 162–3). The precise formal lines of the hedges are counterbalanced by the loose open canopy of the tree and the backdrop of climbers, while the curvaceous round table and chairs lend the garden a quiet elegance.

3 Channelling views and creating vistas is an art that can be used in any size of garden, as illustrated in this design by George Carter. A gap in the hedge frames the vista, marking the start of a progression of devices that automatically leads the eye to the focal point, the urn in the niche. This gives the impression of cultivated elegance in what is otherwise a simple grassed area. Trellis columns, topped here by painted resin pyramids, were used in baroque times instead of yew pyramids, when an instant effect was desired.

1

Celebrating the Picturesque

Inspired by nature and designed by man, the English landscape garden has been copied the world over. These gardens are an idealization of nature, celebrating the beauty of landscapes. Trees, lakes, paths, waterfalls, cascades, streams, and grottos are all carefully arranged to create scenes that please the eye and enhance the site.

The landscape gardener Humphry Repton (1752–1818) was a great exponent of the Picturesque. He enhanced views by drawing the surroundings into a garden, to create a rustic, romantic atmosphere. He noted his ideas and suggestions down in his "Red Books", with before and after sketches (something that we could do now with digital imaging), to check if the suggested design was right. Contrary to popular belief, landscape gardens are not uniquely suited to enormous gardens, nor are they something of the past. Modern interpretations are just as exciting, and suburban and country gardens with mature trees can be transformed by adopting some of the design principles.

1 Using the backdrop of mature trees and a glimpse of what lies beyond, Christopher Bradley-Hole has created an exciting but subtle planting that pleases the eye.

2 Water, as in this moat in the Dutch country-house garden of De Wiersee, takes on a sublime beauty in the early hours of the morning. Lakes and streams were often enhanced in Picturesque landscapes with overhanging trees and gently graded slopes.

3 By resisting the temptation to fill the expanse of lawn, Declan Buckley draws attention automatically to the oak tree in the distance and the seascape beyond.

4 The reflective qualities of sheets of water enhance the landscape, mirroring the surroundings and bringing light into the garden. In this modern Picturesque garden by George Carter, the geometric pool with its dark liner is a counterpoint to the organic flowing forms of the vegetation.

5 Light, weather, and time of day play a vital role in landscape gardens, changing their character and creating different moods. Here, Tom Stuart-Smith has let the background and solitary trees speak for themselves in the early morning mist.

Next spread Pleached lime trees are underplanted with *Geranium endressii*, *Allium hollandicum* 'Purple Sensation', and roses in this garden by Acres Wild.

CASE STUDY

Flower Gardens of a Golden Age

Loose, colourful, and seemingly haphazard flower gardens, with long mixed borders, are one of the most beautiful yet complex forms of garden design to perfect. They are a legacy of the golden age of country gardens, a style that was perfected by Gertrude Jekyll (1843–1932) and Vita Sackville-West (1892–1962) and is synonymous with English gardens and afternoon tea. William Robinson (1838–1935), a great exponent of the flower garden, extolled the virtues of wild flowers in his writings. He encouraged an alternative form of gardening to the Victorian passion for bedding plants and demonstrated it in his own garden at Gravetye Manor.

Robinson purchased Gravetye Manor in West Sussex in 1885 and, over a period of 50 years, he developed the garden to reflect all his principles. Gravetye Manor is now a hotel and its current owners are in the processs of restoring and refreshing the garden under the guidance of Tom Coward, the head gardener.

1 The mixed border along the front wall is built up in a triangular style with low-growing plants at the front and tall plants like *Persicaria orientalis* at the back. Thought has been given to the colour progression that flows in waves through the bed rather than in blocks, with plants being repeated at intervals: in the foreground, purple-flowered *Verbena bonariensis* in front of sedum, with white fleabane (*Erigeron annuus*) in the middle ground around scarlet dahlias.

2 Annuals, such as sunflowers, *Nicotiana* 'White Trumpets', *Cleome hassleriana*, and *Verbena bonariensis*, fill the bed next to the house, creating a forest of flowers.

3 This secluded area is a marvellous example of an English flower garden, at its best when a riot of plants – a mound of purple sage (*Salvia officinalis* 'Purpurascens'), fuchsia-pink cosmos, and tall feathery plume poppies (*Macleaya cordata*) – exists happily side by side.

CASE STUDY
Behind High Walls

Kitchen gardens are experiencing a revival. The walled gardens of large estates and country houses, which were abandoned and closed up in the 1960s, are being rediscovered, transformed, and brought back to life. While many of them follow traditional designs and layouts, a few, like this 0.4-hectare (1-acre) walled garden designed by Julie Toll, are exploring new forms, proving that kitchen gardens can be functional, individual, and exciting.

Traditionally, the size of most walled gardens reflected the size of the house and the quantity of vegetables and fruit that had to be grown to feed the household. Set apart from the house and enclosed by high brick walls, these gardens were the pride and joy of the head gardener but were rarely on show. Now the humble kitchen garden is often the centrepiece of a design.

1 Julie Toll's design for this kitchen garden has picked up on traditional elements, such as freestanding espalier trees and glass domes used as mini greenhouses, and given them a contemporary twist.

2 Instead of parallel, rectangular raised beds, angular forms have been introduced, giving the garden an interesting dynamic quality. This is further emphasized by the use of Cor-Ten™ steel, a weathered steel alloy developed in the US in the 1930s. When exposed to the elements, it develops a protective layer of rust. Available in a range of thicknesses, from wafer-thin up to 50mm (2in), Cor-Ten™ is particularly suited to the outdoors as cladding for freestanding structures or as edging. Here, the patina and russet colour blend well with the old garden wall and brick paths, as well as highlighting the lush, lime-green spring growth.

3 Attention to detail is evident throughout the garden. Instead of being tucked away, this entrance is exquisitely designed. Framed by box buttresses, the metal gate by Arc Angel opens to a path through the orchard, which leads to a large terracotta urn at the end (see also pages 104–5).

UNDER THE SUN

Wanting a touch of the exotic in the garden is nothing new. Over the centuries, the exchange of ideas and plants between different countries has influenced and enriched garden design. During the 19th century, it was *de rigueur* for all larger European gardens to contain within them a Chinese- or Japanese-style garden, filled with new and exciting plants from far-flung places. These days, visitors to the UK often yearn to replicate the English country garden back at home.

1

1 Certain combinations of colour and plants are immediately associated with a particular region. This dusty pink wall, grey-green-leaved olive tree, and soft mauve flowers prompt memories of the Mediterranean, of warmth and southern climes.

2 Paving is just as important as planting in conjuring up a certain look. Here the randomly paved stone path, the yucca-like *Beschorneria yuccoides*, and the olive grove in the background all define this as a Mediterranean garden.

3 The combination of large terracotta pots topped with lush foliage, red latticework gates, and green vegetation speaks of exotic lands, humidity, and warmth. Perhaps surprisingly, this garden, designed by Sue Roscoe-Watts, is not in the Caribbean or Brazil, but in Luxembourg.

Mediterranean Flair

For those living and gardening in a Mediterranean climate, creating a flourishing garden is a challenge, but not an impossibility. The secret is to use plants that thrive in the conditions, and materials that suit their surroundings. In this way, the garden will sit well in the landscape and reflect the natural beauty all around. Introducing Mediterranean style to cooler climates is a different matter. It is all about suggesting a look through using key components and clever plant substitutions.

1 The simplicity of this garden designed by Alithea Johns on the island of Corfu is bewitching. Rosemary pruned into domes forms undulating ground cover against a curtain of olive trees. A not dissimilar effect could be achieved by substituting the olives with apple trees or willows.

2 Mediterranean gardens are particularly attractive to those living in cooler northern latitudes. Here lavender, brick raised beds, gravel, and old, gnarled olive trees give the impression of a Tuscan garden. Olive trees can withstand light frosts and survive in some parts of southern England. In areas with heavy frost, they have to be overwintered in greenhouses or conservatories, like other Mediterranean shrubs such as *Datura* and citrus plants.

3 When designing gardens in a dry climate, it is advisable to use plants that can tolerate the conditions. This Californian garden, designed by Shades of Green, picks up on the idea of lavender fields in Provence and turns it into a sustainable design statement.

4 Terraces and garden rooms typify the gardens of the south of France and Italy. Here, much is made of framing and opening views, drawing in the countryside, and making the garden terrace, which is filled with tree peonies, appear like a precious jewel.

5 Cacti have their own special beauty. When planted against a vibrant background, their different shapes – cushions, cigars, organ pipes – bend and stretch upwards and appear even more distinctive. Cactus gardens can fit in the smallest space, grow on slopes and rocks, and form effective barriers against intruders. In arid climates, they are among the only plants that can survive without irrigation. They deserve to be planted more often.

Spirit of the Far East

Chinese and Japanese gardens have fascinated garden lovers for centuries. Their arrangement of vegetation, paving, and built elements is markedly different from Western gardens, as is the importance of symbolism. The gardens are microcosms, ideal landscapes where the natural world is interpreted through rocks, water, and plants. These personal spaces are dedicated to contemplation and are refuges from the hustle and bustle of the outside world.

Every type of Oriental garden, from the Chinese gardens of the Ming dynasty to Japanese Zen gardens, has its own distinctive character. Built by experts, they represent the highest form of garden art. European interpretations are often simplistic impressions, drawing on key components such as bamboo, fir trees, rocks, water, and stone lanterns.

1 The bamboo planting and impressive statue of a warrior give the illusion that this garden, designed by Kathy Fries, is in China, not the American city of Seattle.

2 This garden designed by Sam Miller has a modern yet distinctly Japanese flavour. The Japanese maple (*Acer palmatum* var. *dissectum*), the elegant bamboo waterspout and wide edging to the pool, the ferns, grasses, and reflective surface of the water, all create a sense of tranquillity.

3 Understanding the symbolism and meaning of plants is the key to designing a Japanese garden. Nothing is left to chance, with everything purposefully placed to create a particular atmosphere. Japanese garden designers are masters who have studied the art and craft of garden-making for years. Maitreya, a Buddist meditation master, has transformed his garden in North Clifton, Nottinghamshire, into an inspiring masterpiece that draws on his knowledge of Japanese gardens.

4 Foliage and form are used to great effect in this Japanese-inspired garden by Acres Wild. Undulating box wraps itself around a *Cornus kousa* var. *chinensis*, forming a plinth to showcase the autumn foliage.

5 The tranquillity of Zen gardens, where everything is reduced to the essential, is mesmerizing. In this Bloedel Reserve garden outside Seattle, raked gravel represents waves lapping against the stone "islands", set in an otherwise calm sea of gravel.

CASE STUDY
Jungle Fever

As we travel further afield, other areas of the Far East, such as Malaysia and Bali, inspire garden designs at home.

A well-designed garden has the ability to transport its owner to a different world that is a refuge and a sanctuary, separate from the grind of daily life. Amir Schlezinger's design for a terrace garden in London achieves just that.

In a compact space no wider than 5m (16½ft), Schlezinger has, through his clever choice of materials and plants, created the illusion of being in a clearing in a tropical jungle. Key to his success is an appreciation of London's microclimate, which is warmer and more humid than the rest of England because it is so built up. This means a different range of plants can be grown, including palms and banana plants, which do very well.

1 Seen from the upper storey of the house, the garden is deceptively simple: a rectangle divided into two sections, with decking on one and gravel on the other, framed by planting. Balau (a tropical hardwood from Asia), with its rich chocolate tones, is used for the decking as well as the bench, and contrasts beautifully with the speckled gravel. The green tones of the vegetation are calming and anything but bland. Plants have been used like sculpture. The oversized fronds of tree ferns (*Dicksonia antarctica*), set against the delicate leaves of *Pittosporum tobira* and spear-like *Phormium*, appear all the more more jungle-like under the thick, towering trunk of the existing tree.

2 A narrow band of box hedging contains, from left to right, *Phormium tenax* 'Variegatum', *Pittosporum tenuifolium* 'Stevens Island', *Aspidistra elatior*, and *Dicksonia antarctica*, with a palm (*Trachycarpus fortunei*) in the background.

3 Looking back towards the house, the view is veiled by the narrow bed of bamboo. The planting seems to envelop and frame the seating area, emphasizing the sense of lushness.

THE NATURAL WAY

Sustainability has become an increasingly important factor in the making of gardens. A rethink is taking place as a result of our increased awareness of the depletion of natural resources, the negative impact of importing products over large distances, and the cost of maintaining and sustaining gardens full of thirsty plants in areas with low rainfall. Water is a precious commodity, and irrigating a garden with mains water is not only expensive but ecologically unsound – provided they are correctly chosen, plants should be able to survive once they are established without any help. Similarly, the use of impermeable paving material not only wreaks havoc with the water table but also creates huge problems with surface-water runoff, putting immense strains on drainage systems. The more surfaces that are paved, the fewer areas there are to soak up precipitation.

The ecological movement of the 1970s drew attention to the value, role, and intrinsic beauty of indigenous vegetation, kick-starting a re-evaluation of gardens as eco-niches. Gardens are part of a chain and the green lungs of a town. Birds, bees, insects, and other wildlife depend on the presence of a certain type of vegetation to survive. This is a finely tuned interdependency that has evolved over time and should be considered in every garden design.

1 Natural gardens have come a long way since the time they were regarded as unkempt wildernesses. Instead of laying a high-maintenance lawn in front of this contemporary house in California, the designers, Shades of Green, opted for a no-mow lawn of bentgrass (*Agrostis pallens*), which does not require irrigation.

2 Natural gardens are not an invention of the 21st century. William Robinson (1838–1935) encouraged the development of natural meadows, and, more recently, Margery Fish (1892–1969) recognized the beauty of wild flowers and that they, too, have a place in the garden. Here, at Pedlinge Court, Kent, *Hesperis matronalis* has self-seeded in the flowerbed, making for a relaxed and uncontrived look.

3 Bog gardens, as here at the Beth Chatto Gardens, Essex, offer a chance to mix native plants with cultivated species, provided that they, like skunk cabbage (*Lysichiton americanus*), thrive in the conditions and require little attention.

4 Boundaries are blurred in this country garden, which is featured on pages 64–5. Sitting beautifully within the landscape, it mirrors its surroundings in the understated design.

CASE STUDY
Using Native Plants

The Fleming Garden in Berkeley, California, is renowned in the landscape world for promoting native plants. Covering less than 0.25 hectares (½ acre) on a steep slope, this exceptional garden is proof that indigenous vegetation can be used to create sustainable and aesthetically pleasing gardens.

The garden is the work of Jenny and Scott Fleming, co-founders of the California Native Plant Society, who purchased the plot of land in 1950 and developed it over a period of more than 50 years. Heavy clay soil, fog, and wind made it difficult to establish a conventional garden. Inspired by the botanical garden at nearby Tilden Park and with advice from the then director, they planted native trees and shrubs, which flourished in otherwise adverse conditions.

1 Slopes and terraces define the garden. The steep gradients were retained with rocks and colonized with a tapestry of plants, all of them native, including *Heuchera maxima*. In total, there are 200 species of native plants to be found here.

2 *Arctostaphylos stanfordiana*, a small tree or large shrub native to California, clings to the slope, growing among the rocks. To the left is live forever (*Dudleya brittonii*), a star-shaped succulent with blue-grey fleshy leaves.

3 The mahogany-coloured branches of *Arctostaphylos* take on a sculptural quality as they arch over the path.

4 As much consideration was given to the selection of paving materials as to the planting. Made of local stone, this path merges into the background.

5 From street level, the slope rises dramatically through woodland to a terrace, then continues still further up into the trees. It is not just the planting that reflects the spirit of the place – the mailbox does, too.

6 Locally sourced lava stone was used for some of the retaining walls. Colonized by ferns (*Polypodium californicum*), the walls have a particularly appealing texture.

CASE STUDY
The Wild Look

Wild gardens are by their very nature relaxed and loose, but this does not mean that they should be left to their own devices. Sensitive management is the key. Designs for these situations should be low-impact, focusing on what is appropriate for the situation, climate, function, size, and budget. While it is possible to create a wild garden in a city, they work better in a rural environment, where gardens tend to be larger and open, often flowing over into the surrounding countryside.

Balancing the designed elements with the natural so that they blend harmoniously is one of the most difficult aspects of garden design. But exceptional gardens can be created if, as in this Irish garden by Dominick Murphy, inspiration is taken from the natural environment.

1 Simple, low-key designs work best in wild gardens. Natural materials, local to the area, should be used wherever possible, as they pick up the tonal nuances of their surroundings. Here, a gravel seating area, edged with timber, is far from intrusive as it blends into the design. Even though the garden is enclosed by a natural stone wall, it nevertheless appears as part of its surroundings.

2 Meadows have a particular beauty, unique to the soil and climate, with an individual mix of species that has evolved over time. Here, shrubby vegetation has been allowed to establish itself, thus enhancing the wild look.

3 A soft grey weathered timber boardwalk is the obvious choice for a path through a boggy part of the garden.

4 Woodland areas and thickets demand low-impact but functional paving, like these natural stone stepping stones.

5 Wild gardens have a charm that comes from not knowing which plants will decide to grow there. Foxgloves (*Digitalis purpurea*), like mulleins (*Verbascum*), are fussy, growing only where they choose. Spontaneous growth is one of the enriching joys of natural gardens.

THE COMPONENTS

STRUCTURE

A garden comprises many layers. Paving and enclosures form the bare bones but rarely is as much thought given to them as to the planting, the soft landscape. Landforms, terraces, and steps are equally important and can underline, or even dictate, the style of a garden. While plants change and grow with the seasons, structural components are permanent and should not be left to chance. Whether functional or ornamental, there are countless designs to choose from.

1 The shape and size of paths, and the materials from which they are made, are integral to a garden's design. They lead us through it, set the tone, and can be design statements in their own right, as in this garden by Tom Stuart-Smith.

2 Enclosing a garden and demarcating ownership is fundamental, but a fence or wall can be so much more than a simple necessity. It can be a significant design element or a piece of art, like this recycled timber fence by James Dunstan.

3 Mastering changes in levels is a challenge. The way in which this is achieved influences not only the look of the garden but how it is used.

Ideally, changes in level should be functional as well as enhancing. They should also relate to the architecture, as garden designer Nan Sinton illustrates here with this natural stone retaining wall in a private garden in the USA.

4 Green architectural elements, such as hedges, are valuable design tools, used in historical as well as contemporary gardens. Hedges can enclose, divide, and define spaces, create "rooms", and also be focal points, as in this private garden.

5

Paving

Hard surfaces, such as drives, paths, and patios, can cover a large proportion of the garden, but rarely do they receive the design attention they deserve. They are the first things to be built, often more out of necessity than aesthetics, with little thought given to what they look like, let alone whether they are fit for purpose or complement the rest of the garden.

A seating zone in a shady woodland area that is used only occasionally requires a different surface treatment from a patio adjacent to the house in continuous use. Similarly, a path to the front door should not be the same as a track through a meadow. Some materials are sharp, precise, and architectural, while others might have a more rustic feel. Reclaimed materials, particularly natural stone and brick, have a patina that is invaluable to some schemes.

1 Patios need not be attached to the house. They can be anywhere in the garden where they catch the sun, as Charlotte Rowe has done here, or, in hotter climates, positioned in the shade, providing protection from the sun.

2 Edging is an important structural element that holds the paving and prevents lateral movement. It can also be a useful design tool and feature, underlining the direction of a path or giving the impression of widening it. In the De Heerenhof garden, Maastricht, a different-coloured brick from that used on the path is laid lengthways, forming a soldier course, to highlight the edge of the path.

3 Mixing materials can be exciting and add interest to a path. Here a straight, wide path through a formal garden, designed by John Brookes and Julie Toll, has been divided into gravel diamonds and brick triangles. The secret with decorative paving is to keep the planting simple and restrained so that they complement each other and do not vie for attention.

4 Paving joints colonized by pretty self-seeding plants, such as *Erigeron karvinskianus*, seen here, can make attractive features. There are many variations on this theme, including thyme walks, where the paving is hardly visible and the creeping plants are the focus.

5 Paths can be opportunities for interesting designs. Here, Rosemary Lindsay has laid paving slabs at an angle, with wide joints, thereby making the narrow path appear much wider than it really is.

7

Paths

A well-designed network of paths gives structure to a garden and sets the tone of the overall design. Paths are far more than a route between two places; they are the backbone of the garden and can also be a major design feature.

Depending on the function and frequency of use, paths have a distinct hierarchy, ranging from a simple walkway through the vegetable garden to narrow tracks across shady areas and stepping stones over water. The type of path determines the width, flow, and surface treatment. The choice of materials and range of patterns is enormous, often bewildering, but simple guidelines can ensure that the material chosen suits both the function and the design.

1 Laying large rectangular slabs in a curve is not easy but it has been achieved exceptionally well in this garden by matching the size of the wedge-shaped grass joints to the radius of the curve.

2 These stepping stones, laid like cushions on the ground, lead to a secluded area of the garden and on their way disappear among the vegetation.

3 Japanese gardens have long been a source of inspiration for the design of paths. This modern interpretation features slate paving stones set in a sea of grey gravel. Simple and effective.

4 Laying pebbles and cobbles is an art. Here, 60–80mm pebbles have been arranged in a random pattern, to create a lively, speckled surface.

5 Paths running around the fringes of a garden act as a frame. In the appropriate colour, they will complement and add interest to the design as a whole.

6 Slippery in the shade and quick to rot when in contact with the soil, timber paths are not always the best solution. However, in this coastal garden, the bleached timber walkway is a fitting choice and is complemented by the planting.

7 Paths running through woodland and along water demand a different treatment from those in an urban setting. Here, a simple timber boardwalk doubles up as a footbridge over a stream.

8 Not all paths need to be paved. Minor paths used infrequently can take the form of tracks or can pick up on the idea of rides – broad paths carved through a wood or, as here, through a meadow. Green tracks, wide enough for two people to walk comfortably side by side, are attractive in country gardens, where the short mown path is set off by long meadow grasses.

9 Even the subtlest of paths can make a design statement. This narrow, single-brick path laid through the meadow at Great Dixter, East Sussex, is more a suggestion of where to walk than a command. Its spontaneous, self-built quality sits well in a country garden.

10 Appearances can be misleading. This path might look as if the slate paddlestones have been simply scattered on the ground but this is a meticulous piece of paving that has taken skill to create. Lower than the surrounding grass and edged with slate kerbing, this Japanese-inspired path is an important design element in the garden, determining the route and the sequence in which the garden is viewed.

11 Narrow stone slabs laid randomly along the path have a random, artistic quality. They enhance what would otherwise be a simple track and provide a strong, directional flow. At the same time, they slow down progression through the garden, forcing the walker to look and feel for the next slab before moving on, thereby drawing attention to the planting on either side.

12 Imaginative paving created with unusual combinations of materials can enrich a garden. Pebbles laid in concrete work particularly well alongside recycled stone in this ornamental and artistic garden path.

13 Paths should always complement the overall design. Here, the straight stone path appears to carve its way through the exuberant, showy planting, which softens its formal lines. The colour of the stone adds a lightness to the scheme.

14 Woodland, shady, and natural gardens require a different sort of path from those that suit formal gardens. They should be low-key, visually unobtrusive but also comfortable and safe to walk on, like this path of bark mulch.

15 Round concrete slabs in different colours and sizes seem to float over this path in a design best suited to a contemporary, arid garden.

1

Front Gardens and Drives

The front garden sets the tone for what the visitor expects to see inside the house. The so-called kerbside effect is all-important when house-hunting: first impressions can make or break a sale. But the front garden is not just for show. As well as accommodating cars, bins, and bikes, it also leads to the front door.

The pressures on this often small patch of land are immense. While suburban front gardens tend to be generous in size, those in towns, cities, and new developments usually have to cram everything into a tiny space. Increasingly, whole areas are being paved over with no regard for the environmental consequences, let alone aesthetics. Legal steps are being taken to mitigate this, and many countries now have by-laws that dictate how much of an area may be paved and with what material. Impermeable surfaces such as asphalt are forbidden in some areas, in a move to reduce surface-water runoff. Planning permission is generally required when paving a front garden for use as hard standing for vehicles. Despite these restrictions, there are many good examples of front garden designs that both meet the environmental criteria and are attractive.

1 Roses over the railings and foxgloves alongside create the feeling of a cottage garden in this front garden in London.

2 Drives and hard standings need to be designed and engineered so they can bear the weight of heavy vehicles, such as SUVs and delivery vans, and also allow room to manoeuvre. Block paving laid in stretcher bond has been used for this generously sized drive by Wilson McWilliam Studio. Careful consideration has been given to the design of the turning circle so that it, too, feels like a part of the garden.

3 This drive might look as though it was built for a garden show but it is real and demonstrates what an inventive London garden owner has managed to achieve. Covered by a pergola, parallel strips of paving lead to the garage. The central strip is a water rill, an interesting alternative to the more usual grass or pebble divide.

1

Patios and Seating Areas

A garden is incomplete without a patio or a seating area. Ranging from a rectangle attached to the house to a secluded area in the far corner of the garden, patios have evolved over recent years to be more than just a space for table and chairs. Location and size are all-important, as is the question of the surface treatment. Different materials can evoke different moods but they should always complement the overall design of the garden and be fit for purpose. At the planning stage, think about the size of your tables and chairs and how they might be configured, as well as the amount of space needed to move around them. Make a note, too, of where and when the sun's rays hit the garden and of any shade cast by trees, fences, and buildings.

1 By opting for two contrasting building materials for the seating areas, set on two different levels, a clear distinction in their use and character has been made in this small contemporary garden. Paved with light grey concrete slabs, the lower patio is crisp and fresh. Its generous proportions will accommodate a larger table and more guests than the upper seating area, which is more intimate. Here, tropical hardwood decking is enveloped by the lush vegetation of bamboo and grasses, complemented by a vibrant Pastil Chair by Eero Aarnio and a lounger.

2 Plain and simple paving can link small areas, to make a space seem larger. Here, the sleek, light grey, natural stone paving also acts as a backdrop to the exuberant planting and statement furniture. The Bubble chair by Eero Aarnio, hanging from the brightly painted moon gate, and the Tulip chair and table by Eero Saarinen are the retro centrepieces, but the overall design of the garden is strong enough to work with different styles of furniture.

3 The strong horizontal lines of this design have been softened by the planting. The paving and boundary treatments all harmonize, making the area appear larger. Like the flooring in a house, patios cannot be changed on a whim. As one of the most expensive items in a garden, they should be built to last and be capable of adapting to changes in taste and use.

4 Timber decking has been a popular surface for patios for many years but getting the design right is not as easy as it might look. The secret, as shown in this garden by Annie Pearce, lies in how the decking is combined with other elements so that a harmonious composition is achieved. The size of the deck is in proportion to the elegant garden furniture, while the horizontal lines of the boards are echoed by the seats, which appear solid but not cumbersome. The planting is constrained, with a multi-stemmed white dogwood (*Cornus kousa* var. *chinensis*) strategically placed, acting like a beacon in among the green vegetation.

5 The regular pattern and the orange-red glow of the recycled bricks give the impression of a rug laid out on the ground. The area is just big enough to accommodate the table and chairs. Laying bricks side by side with crossover joints, also called a jack-on-jack pattern, is only suitable for areas that do not have to support vehicles or other heavy loads. The choice of bricks as a hard surface reflects the contemporary natural elegance of this garden, described on pages 256–7.

6 Patios can be design statements in their own right and the main feature of a garden. Here, a band of lush planting, including blue-flowering *Agapanthus*, frames the central paved area of a courtyard garden designed by Declan Buckley. The dark grey, rectangular paving slabs are subtly patterned and a striking contrast with the foliage, making the greens seem much brighter. This type of treatment is suitable for urban gardens that are also viewed from above. Patios should also be attractive when empty of garden furniture, but when they are in use, it is just as important to prevent them from appearing cluttered.

7 Using contrasting materials can delineate different areas and break up a large area of paving, thereby adding interest, as shown in this small garden designed by Charlotte Rowe. The timber deck patio adjoining the seating area gives way to an area of slate shingle, which is framed on two sides by a band of lighter, contrasting paving. Restricting the colour palette to different shades of grey means that the various materials do not jar or appear too busy. Instead, a harmonious surface is created, with the focus on texture.

1

Matching Paving Materials to Function

There are many different paving materials available, but some are better suited than others to a particular function. Being guided by what will work on a practical level can prevent costly mistakes. Climate, function, and level of skill are key factors to consider.

Some materials are better at withstanding frost than others, which is a particular consideration in more northern latitudes. Appreciating the function of a surface is important when selecting the material and the bond (laying pattern). The purpose of hard paving is to provide a clean, even, foot-friendly, stable, and quick-draining surface. Areas that have to support heavy loads and vehicle movement are subject to a different set of design criteria from those used solely by pedestrians. The more a surface is used, the stronger the paving has to be. The strength of unit paving depends on the bond and how well the units – concrete, brick, or natural stone – interlock and carry loads. Correct and appropriate construction is essential.

1 Flagstones need to be of a certain thickness to be viable outdoors. A useful rule of thumb is that the larger the surface area of the flagstone, the thicker it should be. Like all paving, stepping stones or lengths of paving with wide grass joints should be bedded correctly if they are not to tilt and crack. Sedimentary stone, like the sandstone used in this London garden by Sara Jane Rothwell, might, depending on its provenance, be more susceptible to frost damage than dense natural stone such as granite (see also page 85).

2 Naturalistic country gardens call for a different type of paving from formal or contemporary gardens. Timber decking is really the only choice for boggy areas, where other paving would disappear.

3 Garden paths are usually constructed solely for pedestrian use and so can be paved in a variety of ways. Here, bricks in a diagonal herringbone pattern are contained by a row of the same bricks laid on edge.

4 Organic flowing forms or amorphous shapes are difficult to pave with unit paving. Loose material such as gravel, shown along the drive in Bryan's Ground, Herefordshire, is ideal for such situations.

4

Natural Stone

Natural stone has been used for paving for thousands of years. In the past, it was the norm to have local stone for buildings and paving alike, and imported stone only for prestigious projects. As a consequence, each region developed its own paving language and skill set to work natural stone. Today, it is still the material of choice but cost, availability, and the lack of skilled labour have turned it into a luxury item.

Durability, size, and colour are the prime concerns when selecting stone. Not every type is suitable for outdoors. Granite, basalt, and gneiss are among the hardest, while the hardness and durability of sedimentary stone, such as sandstone, limestone, and slate, vary from quarry to quarry and region to region. Broadly speaking, stone is available as paving slabs and setts, cobbles, pebbles, fieldstones, and gravel. Colours range from greys and creams to yellow-browns and varying intensities of red. As a rule of thumb, the more exotic and brighter the colour of the stone, the less likely it is to be able to withstand cold winters. The more a stone is worked, the greater the cost, but good stone holds its value, as proven by the constant demand for recycled stone.

1 Slate is an attractive material, available as small, plate-like paving, tiles, paddlestones, and gravel. Here, slate slabs are surrounded by a pattern of slate laid on its side.

2 Limestone is sold primarily as paving slabs, as used here in a design by Amir Schlezinger, and occasionally as setts. The main attraction is its light creamy colour but checks should be made before using it in areas with heavy frost.

3 York stone paving and gravel complement each other in this garden designed by del Buono Gazerwitz Landscape Architecture.

4 Natural stone cut in a variety of sizes has been used to great effect in this garden designed by Julie Toll. The contrast in colour between the light oppdal quartzite from Norway and the dark Chinese basalt is quite distinct and will endure as both materials darken.

Setts, Cobbles, and Pebbles

The small, handy size of setts, cobbles, and pebbles makes them particularly appealing for use in the garden. Paths and patios can be paved in all sorts of designs and patterns, to lend the garden a certain individuality.

Cobbles and pebbles were used for some of the earliest paving and have a distinctive egg-like shape. Both are sold graded according to size: pebbles, 20–40mm; cobbles, 40–90mm. On no account should pebbles be taken from beaches or riversides. Setts are cubes cut from quarried stone and have historically been used to create some of the most beautiful paving. Their sizes are regulated and categorized as mosaic (40–60mm), small (80–100mm), and large (150–220mm).

1 Cobbles are particularly suited to random patterns and amorphous forms. Here, Lucy Sommers has used contrasting colours to create a dramatic design.

2 Black and white pebbles have been meticulously sorted and laid to create an intricate decorative pattern, designed by Michael Gough. Beautiful examples of old paving can be found in towns along the Mediterranean, where beach pebbles were once the local building material.

3 Using graded pebbles of a similar shape and size is essential for pebble paving patterns. The chequerboard effect here has been enhanced by turning the direction of the rows in each square by 90 degrees.

4 Sett paving is popular in Europe where there are still skilled craftsman capable of laying the intricate patterns. Each sett has a distinct face, which is smoother than the other sides of the cube. When laid with the correct width of joints in the appropriate pattern and a prepared base, setts make a firm, durable, and aesthetically pleasing surface. While this example, in the De Heerenhof garden, Maastricht, of three rows of large setts, laid side by side, might be suitable for a garden path, it is not recommended for other situations. Joints should be staggered for a strong bond.

5 Small setts have been laid in concentric rings to create a circular seating area at De Heerenhof. Setts are only roughly the same size, so it is possible for the trained eye to select the right stone for each position in the circle without the need for large, wedge-shaped joints.

Brick and Clinker Pavers

Bricks were traditionally manufactured in areas where no local supply of natural stone existed. They blend especially well in gardens, their warm reds and soft browns complementing the vegetation. Their uniform size makes them easier to lay than setts on a prepared base, and there is a pattern to suit every situation, from drives to narrow paths.

Not all building bricks can be used outdoors. Constant contact with the ground and exposure to the elements means that only specially manufactured outdoor pavers, such as clinker, known as engineering brick pavers in the UK, are suitable.

1 Instead of being laid at right angles, these pavers in stretcher bond are in panels parallel to the direction of the path. It is a clever optical trick by Jane Brockbank and David Mikhail Architects that appears to lengthen the view to the house.

2 Farmyard bricks have been laid in a block pattern along this path. The encroaching planting and the elements have worn the bricks down, giving a rustic appearance.

3 This reclaimed brick paving has a similar optical quality to clinker, which has been fired at a high temperature and is denser and tougher than brick. Clinker often has bluish hues or a flamed surface, which suits an urban setting.

4 A wide brick path laid in a basket-weave pattern contrasts well with the more contemporary seating area designed by Chris Ghyselen.

5 Both brick and clinker can be mixed with other materials. Julie Toll has added rectangles of bricks to a patchwork path, picking up the bright shades of red hot poker (*Kniphofia*) in the border.

6 This path laid with slim pavers in stretcher bond appears even more vibrant set against the dark vegetation and white hydrangea.

7 What could have been a dull, endless promenade has been transformed by Acres Wild. A wide band of natural stone frames and dissects the broad path at intervals. The panels are filled with bricks laid in herringbone bond, which reduces the scale and adds a rhythm to the path.

8 Herringbone is a versatile bond suitable for drives, patios, and even narrow paths.

1

Concrete

For many years, concrete was regarded as a poor relation of natural stone and brick, which it tried to imitate and replicate. New concrete products and innovative uses have prompted its renaissance, and concrete is now recognized as a material with great potential in the contemporary garden.

The advantages of the manufacturing process guarantee consistency in colour and shape. As with all products exposed to the elements, colours will fade over time but the advantage of concrete lies in its versatility. Concrete is available as unit paving and paving slabs in a variety of sizes and finishes. The bonds are the same as for natural stone and brick.

1 Concrete lends itself to being moulded into interesting and unusual shapes. The High Line in New York, designed by James Corner Field Operations, Diller Scofidio + Renfro, and Piet Oudolf, is an exemplary project, particularly in the use of paving. Here, linear, finger-like paving appears to be swallowed by the vegetation, as the tracks of the old railway once were. The speckles add an attractive extra dimension.

2 Polished concrete is a recent innovation, used indoors for worktops and flooring. In a garden, it is perhaps more suitable as a finish for benches and tables than for paving, which needs to be non-slip.

3 The clean lines of this paving, which could equally well have been paved with concrete slabs, complement Amir Schlezinger's contemporary design. The attention to detail is striking. Awkward shapes and junctions with the adjoining surfaces have been avoided by using perfectly fitting units.

4 In this garden designed by Shades of Green, large concrete slabs laid in a grid, with wide gravel joints, make a strong design statement, while fulfilling practical considerations – surface water runs off through the joints, avoiding the build-up off puddles. Although patios and paths can be paved in this way, it is unsuitable for surfaces used by vehicles. Large concrete slabs for supporting heavier weights are available but they must be laid with closer joints. Quality paving comes at a price, and the maxim that "the larger the slab, the higher the price" applies.

Aggregates and Specials

Crushed stone, gravel, and shingle have a long history of use in private gardens. Decorative yet functional, these aggregates come in a wide range of colours and sizes, to suit any design. They are also easy to lay and can take on any shape, regardless of size.

In recent years there has been an increase in the use of aggregates and materials like ceramic shards as decorative ground cover. A distinction has to be made between this and surfaces that are walked or driven on, which is reflected in the size of the material and construction techniques.

1 Gravel is the ideal surface for a seating area in this Californian garden designed by Shades of Green. It is unobtrusive, fit for purpose, and picks up the nuances of colour in the surrounding walls.

2 Metal grilles, commonly found as covers over shafts, have been used by Nigel Dunnett as inventive paving material.

3 Gravel can be combined with other types of paving to produce interesting effects. Here, cream paving and dark grey setts are framed and highlighted by dark gravel in a design by Michel Bras, Eric Raffy, and Philippe Villeroux.

4 Light speckled gravel echoes the relaxed nature of this Acres Wild country garden. Selecting the right aggregate is not easy; it is worth getting samples beforehand and trying them in situ.

5 Some paving designs are works of art. Michele Osborne created this colourful example with the imaginative use of brick and stone setts in different sizes, interspersed with ceramic shards.

6 Pebbles and bespoke fired and glazed ceramic "pebbles" have been masterfully laid to give a unique character to a Lucy Sommers scheme. The frost-hardiness of certain materials can be an issue, so check before using in cold areas.

7 Simple, elegant, and refined, this gravel path in June Blake's garden in County Wicklow has been divided by a weathered strip of Cor-Ten™ steel, sunk into the ground. The lawn edging is also Cor-Ten™.

8 Different-sized stone slabs laid in a random pattern, with gravel joints, have an aesthetic all of their own. This simple paving solution has stood the test of time and is suitable for both traditional and contemporary gardens.

4

Timber

Readily available as boarding, decking, blocks, and mulch and bark chippings, timber is a versatile and popular paving material. The ease of construction and the relatively low cost are factors that have added to its appeal. Longevity is a problem, but the correct choice of timber and good construction go a long way towards extending its life expectancy.

1 Timber decking evokes images of lakes, seas, and jetties stretching out into the water. It works best when cantilevered or supported from below the water so that it appears to be floating, as in this design by Chris Ghyselen. Hardwoods make the best decking material but their high cost means that impregnated softwoods are often used instead. Imported tropical hardwood should only be purchased from approved and licensed sources.

2 Decking is used increasingly on roof gardens where weight is an issue and construction depths are restricted. In this Sara Jane Rothwell design, the raised beds and built-in bench are also made from timber. Set off by the planting, this scheme strikes a contemporary note.

3 Timber in direct contact with the ground is liable to rot quickly. In shady woodland gardens, logs used as edging – round log paving would seem the logical choice – can underline the natural setting. However, they do become slippery in damp conditions. Here, the log paving has taken on the quality of a work of art, highlighting the junction of paths.

4 Wood and bark chippings come in a variety of grades and colours. As well as being used as a mulch on flowerbeds, they are ideal for tracks through woods, where the ground is liable to get muddy and an informal path is required. It is important to use the right grade of material; fine, powdery chippings are just as unsuitable as large pieces. When spread, the wood chippings have a soft, spongy, bouncy quality. They can take up any shape but are difficult to contain, as they tend to stray from the path. This is not a problem in natural gardens, as in this design by Annie Pearce, but it does become irritating if a formal look is desired.

STEPS AND RAMPS

Linking levels is a challenge in any garden. The layout and position of steps and ramps can make or break a design. If well planned and constructed, they are more than a means of moving from one level to another – they can underline the character of a garden and be a valuable design tool. Practicalities govern the design. Dimensions used in buildings cannot be used outside: risers (height of a step) must be lower, and treads (depth of a step) wider, for comfort and safety.

1 Steps in country and woodland gardens can be informal but also functional. Here, ramped steps, made from chestnut boards, master the incline.

2 The design and materials used for steps close to the house should match its architecture. Bricks are used here for the steps, stringer (the supporting and enclosing structure of steps), and path. If wide enough, steps can be used for displaying plants or even sitting on. Stringers lend a formal note and are a design element in themselves.

3 Leading from the basement level of the house into the garden, this flight of steps is a piece of architecture, graceful and contemporary. It also acknowledges that outdoor steps need to be lower and deeper than those in a building. A useful rule for deciding measurements for risers and treads, based on the length of a stride (600mm/2ft), is: h (height) + d (depth) + h = 600mm. Maths is unavoidable in step design and working with actual measurements is better than guesswork.

4 Timber-framed stepped landings negotiate both the height difference and the change in direction and are absolutely in keeping with the garden style.

Matching Steps to the Garden

Depending on the character of the garden, steps can be either unobtrusive or an important feature. Whichever option is chosen, the dimensions of the risers and treads need to be consistent and, above all, steps should be recognizable as such.

1 Leaving the edge of the slab at the bottom of this short flight of steps uncut and rough is unexpected and changes the look completely.

2 Logs held in place by stakes have been laid at equal distances following the contours of the grass slope, to create ramped steps.

3 Bedding rocks so that they appear natural is an art in itself, while constructing craggy steps is a matter of selecting the right stone for the right place, maintaining, as far as possible, a uniform height for the risers. These steps blend in perfectly with the rugged look of the rock garden.

4 By leaving the face of the block quartzite steps rough, Julie Toll has achieved an elegant cragginess, as she has also done with the steps in photographs 1 and 5. The deep treads and low height give the steps a leisurely generosity.

5 Block steps hewn out of a single stone can be cut to size to suit the design. Seen from above, these treads have a sturdy quality, with the planting acting as a stringer, flanking and enclosing the steps.

6 Without trying, these wide ramped steps are a focal point. By playing with the rhythm of the treads and varying the surface material of the ramps from gravel to grass, June Blake has achieved an interesting rustic effect.

7 The relationship of planting to steps is vital in a design. The tall grasses envelop these steps, underlining the natural character of this Acres Wild design.

8 Steps present challenges and opportunities. On the opposite side of the pool shown in photograph 1, a different character has been achieved by high-specification, bespoke ipe hardwood steps. Set at an angle, they echo the stone steps in the front garden.

1

Outdoor Staircases

Long flights of steps have a special quality and, by virtue of their sheer mass, can be a major feature of the garden. Ideally, they should be interrupted by landings, for a chance to catch one's breath and take in the view, but they should not appear daunting to climb. Steps in historic gardens are a great source of inspiration.

1 Links between the house and the garden are important. In this design by Sara Jane Rothwell, a flight of steps leads from the basement to the garden. Light colours enhance what could potentially have been a dark space, and vertical planting provides an optical link to the garden.

2 Timber steps can have their own elegance. These long, wide steps, by Anthony Paul Landscape Design, are staggered across the slope, making a change from the usual straight runs.

3 By using the same stone – honed basalt – for the coping as for the paving and the treads, Charlotte Rowe has created a sense of unity in this sleek design. Dark grey, almost black, mirrors have been added to the risers, giving a transparent quality to the steps.

4 Treads and stringers (the retaining edges that hold and support steps) can be opportunities for colour statements. Stuart Craine has paved these treads in natural stone, while the risers and surrounds are rendered and painted in a striking fuchsia-pink, a colour picked up in the planting.

5 Cantilevered steps have an undeniable elegance. The chunky timber treads in this design by Christopher Bradley-Hole appear to be floating, casting a deep shadow that masks the concrete supports.

6 Solid concrete block steps lead up to the front door. The plants on either side have substantially narrowed the width of the steps and at the same time softened the harsh nature of the concrete.

7 The walls, paving, and steps are all constructed from the same material, giving a wonderful coherence to the design.

1

Steps as Design Elements

Urban gardens, particularly those in inner cities, are often spread over different levels. The addition of a basement, to create additional living space, introduces a whole new set of issues. Designing access to all levels of the garden is, however, an opportunity for interesting designs. In these confined spaces, steps are more than a means to move between different heights; they are an integral part of the garden and a design feature in their own right.

1 Viewed from the reception room, the concrete steps into this garden designed by Modular have taken on a sculptural quality. Backed by the lush greens of the bamboo screen, their grey colour appears darker and more intense. Altering the direction after the first three steps by 90 degrees sends out an invitation to explore the garden, as well as making it seem larger than it really is.

2 Larger gardens have the space to accommodate more generously proportioned steps. In this garden designed by the Wilson McWilliam Studio, they have an aesthetic as well as a functional purpose: they are a link from one area of the garden to the other, and their design reflects the refined contemporary tone of the garden. Made of natural stone and with low risers and deep treads, these wide, elegant steps flow seamlessly into the pool garden. Colours are muted and the focus is on the fin-like sculpture, carved out of Kilkenny limestone, by Dominic Welch, which rises out of the planting in the distance.

3 Strong horizontal lines and light colours dominate this design for a private garden designed by Jane Brockbank and David Mikhail Architects. The seating area and planting beds are staggered, with each level framed by white bricks with grey lime mortar set on edge, giving the design a strong linear quality. The block-like steps are hardly visible and merge into the vegetation, so that the seating area appears to be floating. The garden beyond, framed by the brickwork, could be a painting or a mirage, as here, too, the step is hidden from view.

ENCLOSURES AND BARRIERS

The garden fence marks ownership, protects from intruders, and gives a sense of privacy. In the past, it would have been built of whatever material was to hand: stone, timber, brick, or plants. But an enclosure is much more than a functional barrier; it is a form of secondary architecture that can lend style and character to a property. It can be slick or rustic, grand or functional; a fence, railings, a wall, a hedge, or even a mixture; it can make a statement or just blend in.

1 Openings in fences, walls, and railings are just as important as the enclosures themselves. They mark the entrance and should be secure yet inviting, and sometimes, like the French *grande grille*, imposing. Domestic versions are less dramatic but can be equally beautiful, as in this garden, which is described on pages 50–1.

2 A wall topped by a fence is given a contemporary treatment. The need to shut oneself off is tempered in some areas by local laws and planning regulations that limit the height and type of enclosure. It is worth making enquiries about this at the design stage.

3 Regional and historical examples of fencing can be inspiring, like this picket fence with a tall arch over the entrance. Thinking about how an enclosure will appear from the outside, as well as from the inside, should also be taken into account.

4 Barriers within the garden can delineate spaces, dividing the garden into rooms with different functions. Hedges are ideal for this purpose, with a range of species to suit every type of enclosure, from low to high.

1

Fences

Fences can complement and enhance a property, combining function and design. They are versatile, easy to construct, and available in a wide range of prefabricated units, to suit a variety of locations, from rural to inner city, and old buildings as well as new. All fences create barriers and, like a veil, arouse curiosity. They should not be designed in isolation but with regard to the look of the garden as a whole.

Inspiration can be found in open-air rural craft museums, such as Glenleiten in Germany, historic gardens, and even the suburbs built in the late 19th century. Certain regions, such as New England, have distinct styles of fencing. Contemporary designs are often an interpretation of traditional designs but, whatever the style, all fences rely on good construction techniques.

1 Hurdles are one of the earliest forms of fencing, originally used for the temporary enclosure of livestock. The units, which can be picked up and transported with ease, are staked in the ground. Woven primarily in willow or hazel, these barriers can be used as instant screens, to hide bins and other unsightly objects, or as temporary fencing that will have rotted away by the time newly planted hedges have matured.

2 Fences around country cottages can have a rustic, improvised nature. This simple post-and-rail fence has been supplemented by a lower one made of twigs, evoking a picturesque charm. The fence marks the boundary but is no barrier to livestock, unlike the split oak fences that were traditionally used by cottagers in the 19th century.

3 Ropes strung through timbers have a nautical feel, which is fitting for this coastal garden designed by Jo Thompson. In certain situations, being able to see out of a garden is more important than barricading oneself in.

Pickets and Latticework

Picket fences are one of the most popular types of enclosure. They have been used for centuries and were originally developed from the simple paling fence, in which pointed stakes were nailed to rails. Painted gentrified versions of common garden enclosures used in medieval times are to be found in the front gardens of villages and suburbs throughout the world.

In its simplest form, latticework is made of poles, laths, or battens nailed diagonally or at right angles, to form rectilinear panels supported by a frame, which is then fixed to posts. It can be freestanding or mounted on walls and is often painted.

1 Traditional country fences can inspire contemporary designs. Here, the principles of cleft oak fencing have been reworked in a garden by Cleve West and Johnny Woodford. The distance between the timbers is in proportion to their width, an important factor in fence design. The top of the fence has been shaped to produce a pleasing wave effect.

2 Modern latticework, a sophisticated form of garden carpentry, comes in a range of designs that are often made to order to suit a particular garden. Pattern books from the end of the 19th century are a mine of ideas for the contemporary garden.

3 Picket fences come in an astonishing range of sizes and designs, given that their basic construction of two parallel timbers supporting pickets of equal distance apart is so simple. The timbers can be shaped in a variety of ways: rounded, as shown here, angled, spear-shaped, and more. The posts can be simple, turned, or capped, lending further variety to the design.

4 This bright pink-striped fence in a Hampton Court Palace Flower Show garden, designed by Wendy Smith and Fern Alder, reinterprets the design language of a picket fence, bringing a luminosity and fresh appeal to the space. Constructed from strips of perspex, it might not be very durable but it is an interesting solution.

5

6

All Boarded Up

Close-board fencing is used increasingly in cities and new housing developments, where gardens are small and privacy is paramount. However, in some areas it is not allowed to be more than 1.5m (5ft) high. Check for any local restrictions at the ideas stage.

1 Timber battens placed close together make for a strong horizontal pattern. Fencing like this, designed by Charlotte Rowe, can be used to clad unattractive features such as firewalls and give cohesion to a design. Leaving larger gaps above eye level is a clever ploy, allowing light to filter through.

2 Wattle fencing has been rediscovered. Imaginative variations on the theme, some inspired by Japanese nightingale fences made from upright lengths of bamboo bunched together, have become increasingly popular in gardens, particularly where low-cost and quick-to-build options are required.

3 Incorporating existing enclosures, such as walls, without incurring massive costs can be a problem in the gardens of older houses. Here, Sara Jane Rothwell has painted the existing brick wall white, to complement the paving, and fixed a horizontal close-board fence made of balau, a hardwood, on top. Pleached hedging around the perimeter softens the fence and adds another layer of privacy.

4 By changing the direction of the timbers, this fence has been given an interesting structure and appears less dominating.

5 Fences, particularly when they are high and close-board, can be claustrophobic and prison-like. In this well-considered, contemporary design by Christopher Bradley-Hole, the hard lines and mass of the fence are softened by the planting in and outside the garden, and also by the paving. The fence doubles up as a backrest for the benches and as a backdrop for the water feature slotted in the fence to the left.

6 In a garden designed by Annie Pearce, light filters through the vertical slats of the high, dark fence, making a pleasant and interesting backdrop.

Railings

Railings are sophisticated versions of fences, made out of wrought iron or, more commonly, cast iron. Expensive and elegant, they trigger visions of French chateaux, grand houses, and smart London squares.

Mass production in the foundries during the Industrial Revolution brought railings within the grasp of the burgeoning middle classes. Catalogues were produced offering a range of cast-iron fence components – posts, pickets, and gates – in all manner of ornamental forms, to suit every taste. New railings are rarely made nowadays. There is more focus on the restoration of existing railings and hunting through architectural salvage yards for parts that can be incorporated into modern designs.

1 Highly ornamental scalloped railings, here topped by wave-like spears, are often painted to match the colours of the house, as at Sezincote, Gloucestershire. A similar design to the railings shown was mass-produced at the end of the 19th century as a wire-mesh fence. It sold widely all over Europe and can still be found in some Viennese suburbs. At that time, enclosures were barriers that denoted status as much as ownership and they were seen as an integral part of the architecture of a house.

2 Interesting modern fences that work as attractive screens as well as fences tend to be one-off designs. This horizontal galvanized metal artistic composition was designed by Alison Sloga for a garden at a Hampton Court Palace Flower Show.

3 Railings can protect as well as enclose. The rows of railings outside certain early Victorian houses on London streets are not merely demarcations of property but also protection for passers-by, to prevent them from falling down basement stairwells. They are durable and strong, as are railings on balconies and roof gardens. In this garden, Christopher Bradley-Hole has combined a staggered steel railing with a planter that enhances and softens the barrier.

5

Walls

Enclosed by stone or brick, a walled garden is the ultimate secret garden, with a unique atmosphere. The look of a wall is determined by the material used and the style of construction. Experienced stonemasons and bricklayers are worth their weight in gold, as they can translate a design idea into reality, as well as adding their own particular touch.

All freestanding walls must be stable and safe, built on foundations and topped by coping stones to divert rainwater. High and long walls must be built to the specifications of a structural engineer. Brick walls may require piers and supports, which can also be a design feature. Traditionally, wherever stone was readily available, it was always used in gardens. Regional styles of field walls are a good source of ideas for gardens, as dressed stone of unified shape and size, known as ashlar, is beyond the budget of most garden owners.

1 In a garden designed by Julie Toll, plate-like natural stone has been expertly laid and finished off with quarried sawn stone, giving an elegant finish to the wall.

2 Local stone and local expertise were used to build this wall, which blends perfectly with the surroundings but would sit equally well with formal planting. The planting and decoration give a contemporary feel.

3 The beautiful rhythm and pattern of dry-stone walls rely on expert construction, but the design details are important, too. Here, Annie Pearce has chosen Guiting, an oolitic limestone from the north Cotswolds, for the stone bench, which echoes the coping and picks up the golden tones of the weathered and newly quarried stone wall.

4 Brick walls have a beauty about them, even when they are stained with white patches of leaching salts. This example has a simple coping of bricks laid on edge in a soldier course.

5 Gabions – metal baskets filled with stones – were once only found supporting river banks. Now they are used in all sorts of ways in the garden, including as an unusual bench when topped with a plank of wood or a large slab of stone. Here, Stuart Craine has used a stack of gabions to create a striking focal point.

6

7

6 When done sympathetically, mixing wall materials can produce interesting and individual designs. Here, Arterra Landscape Architects have used large stones, with a rustic, fresh-from-the-quarry look, that reflect the locality but do not break the bank. Irregular in size, the pieces of stone give the wall the appearance of a jigsaw puzzle. The face of the stone has been worked, to give a smooth surface, but the edges have been left raw, which contrasts well with the rendered wall alongside, in just the right shade of dusty pink.

7 Rendered walls are frequently dull and unexciting but, when carefully thought out, they can become an integral part of a design, even a highlight, as François Valentiny demonstrates here. Bold red and orange walls create a warmth that contrasts well with the vegetation and neutral paving. Simplicity is the key to this design, as is an appreciation of shapes and forms.

8 These chunky quarried stones have a powerful quality, reminiscent of ancient Roman polygonal walls. Accompanied by a lawn in front and free-flowing ornamental grasses behind, this retaining wall by the landscape architect Jacques Wirtz has a timeless quality. A similar effect was created by Wirtz in Jubilee Park, London, using split limestone blocks.

9 Although modern, this design by Shades of Green has an earthy feel to it. The various elements – the rendered and concrete walls resembling rammed earth, the papyrus grass, and trough-like basin with trickling water – combine to evoke warm, dry climates.

1

Hedges

These green walls of the garden have developed considerably since the time they were the default option for field boundaries. Today, hedges are as much a statement as a barrier, a valuable design tool that can shape and define a garden.

A garden is not a garden without a hedge of some kind in it. Different hedging plants can be used to evoke a particular era or style: privet is a symbol of suburbia; tall, clipped hornbeam or beech is an essential component of the French baroque garden; yew is synonymous with Tudor times and topiary; hawthorn and field maple introduce a rustic touch. Field hedges are an essential part of the English countryside and, like their historic counterparts, are a great source of ideas.

1 Maintenance is the key to growing a successful garden hedge. Knowing which plant to use, and how and when to clip it, is vital. Left to grow unrestrained, every hedge will become unkempt and unrecognizable. Seen in profile, cut hedges have a distinct box shape, but tall hedges should taper slightly and be broader at the bottom than the top. *Thuja* and *Chamaecyparis* have both had a bad press in recent times, but they do have desirable qualities. Provided they are cut regularly, they make worthwhile hedges, as illustrated by this *Thuja plicata* hedge in Jenny Raworth's quintessential English garden in Twickenham, outside London.

2 *Elaeagnus macrophylla*, an evergreen shrub, makes a good architectural hedge on chalk-free soils. Like many evergreens, it is susceptible to frost, winds, and leaf burn from the strong winter sun reflected on the snow. In climates where it thrives, as here in the gardens at Anglesey Abbey, Cambridgeshire, it is best used as architectural subdivisions.

3 Hornbeam (*Carpinus betulus*) is a versatile, deciduous hedging plant that can be kept at a range of heights. Like beech (*Fagus sylvatica*), its dry brown leaves hang on the plant in winter until new growth appears in spring, which gives it a very attractive appearance. Instead of cutting the tops of hedges flat, they can be undulated, to produce a sculptural effect, as in Chris Ghyselen's garden.

4 Hornbeam (*Carpinus betulus*) is used as a slender boundary hedge and a divider in this small London garden, which is featured on page 309. When planting, there is a choice of staggering the plants in two rows for a thicker, more substantial hedge, or placing them in a single line. Specially prepared hedge plants are available from good nurseries in sizes from 1m to 2.5m (3–8ft) in height.

5 *Photinia*, with its characteristic bright red-orange new growth, is increasingly popular as a hedge in areas with mild climates. The name derives from the Greek *photeinos*, meaning shiny, an apt description of this naturally erect evergreen shrub, which has an almost tropical, exotic air about it, as shown in this design by Paul Southern.

6 Yew (*Taxus baccata*) is one of the most common hedging plants in northern European gardens. Once established, it grows surprisingly quickly, provided it has the right conditions, creating a dense hedge that can be clipped into any shape, to create interesting pieces of topiary. Here, at Cothay Manor, Somerset, the plants on either side of the gap have been trained with the help of a frame, to create an arch. Yews are resilient and can adapt to any style, being as much at home in a suburban front garden as in a country house or cottage garden.

7 Hedges can melt into the background or draw the eye. Cut straight, this laurel (*Prunus laurocerasus*) hedge at Elton Hall, Cambridgeshire, would just be a backdrop, but scalloped and clipped into peaks, it becomes a striking part of the design. In spite of its largish leaves, laurel can be pruned into shape.

8 Two hedges, two different effects. Precisely clipped yew hedges define this garden room in Penshurst Place, Kent, while *Berberis thunbergii* f. *atropurpurea* 'Atropurpurea Nana', with its vibrant colour and prickly growth, is used as a low hedge around rose beds. Other useful species for medium-sized architectural hedging are field maple (*Acer campestre*) and *Cornus mas*. Both are compact deciduous hedges, growing to around 1m (3ft) tall. Privet (*Ligustrum vulgare*) is regarded as old-fashioned, but this hardy, deciduous to evergreen quick-growing hedge should not be disregarded. Hollies – the common holly (*Ilex aquifolium*) is the best known – have several species suitable for hedging in urban and rural situations. Flowering hedges make a loose, unstructured barrier and need space to flourish. They are most successful in larger or country gardens, where a more relaxed style is desired.

Making an Entrance

Garden gates can be imposing or understated merely by virtue of their style. Their design follows a distinct hierarchy, according to function and status. A main gate should be immediately recognizable as such, while a side entrance can be discreetly tucked away. Whatever the role, a gate should always be in keeping with the design of the garden boundary, be easy to use, and be fitted with appropriate ironmongery.

1 Internal gates from one garden area to another can be kept simple or used as an opportunity to reflect the style of the garden. In traditional country gardens, a painted door in the brick wall might be fitting, but in this contemporary garden, the gate by Jamie Fobert is a work of art and a beautiful backdrop to the planting.

2 Even simple gates can frame views. This picket fence extends as an arch over the single gate in a garden designed by Theresa-Mary Morton.

3 Hung between brick pillars, this 19th-century metal garden gate manages to be both imposing and elegant. Similar designs can be found in architectural salvage yards, adding flair if used in the right setting.

4 Gates within a garden can be individual and whimsical, like this "garden tool" gate by George Carter.

5 As pieces of secondary architecture, gates are style statements. They can lend gravitas or lightness to a scheme and be more than just an entrance. This delicate wrought-iron gate, embellished with leaves, frames the view of the distant urn, inviting the viewer to enter the garden.

6 A simple picket gate framed by a yew arch leads into the front garden of Shandy Hall, Yorkshire.

7 One gate, two sides. Considering what a gate looks like from both sides makes for good design, as Sue Roscoe-Watts shows here. Lush planting, Oriental in design, emphasizes the exotic appeal of this gate. Whatever the design, gates should be wide enough to fit wheelbarrows and mowers.

8 The design of a gate says a lot about the property and what the house might look like. A picket gate, complete with turned posts, hints at understated country charm.

Space Dividers and Eye-Catchers

Moving from one part of the garden to another has an element of drama and surprise to it. Even the smallest garden can be divided into different areas. The trick is to have continuity of design and to treat the garden like good music, with crescendos and quiet pieces.

Rhythm and pace are just as important in garden design as in music. Announcing, "here is something special, pay attention" is something that Chinese garden designers mastered during the Ming dynasty. Uneven ground slowed the pace, forcing the walker to pay attention. The reward was beautiful paving full of symbols, or a view that could only be seen from that exact spot. Gardens are, to an extent, like walk-in sculptures, and appreciating how spaces will work and interlink is one of the most exciting aspects of their design.

1 Moon gates in Chinese gardens are full of symbolic meaning. They frame and announce that a special garden lies ahead. The circle represents heaven, and by walking through the opening the visitor enters a different world. Many Western gardens have incorporated this form as an eye-catching feature. Here, in the Old Vicarage, Gloucestershire, the opening divides and links the kitchen garden to the pleasure garden, indicating a change from work to leisure, from functional to ornamental. The details – the slightly raised step, the brick paving, and the draping rose – all enhance the view.

2 Transparent dividers, like this innovative copper screen by Heather Appleton, are particularly attractive.

3 Cor-Ten™ steel is the material of choice in many contemporary gardens. Whenever and wherever it is used, it catches the eye. In this private garden designed by del Buono Gazerwitz Landscape Architecture, it is used as a screen, paired with Faye Toogood's contemporary Spade Chair and concrete bowl.

4 Even the tiniest garden can incorporate divisions. Another moon gate, in a contemporary design by Ana Sanchez-Martin, creates a different effect from the gate opposite (1), but the threshold still heralds a change in pace and mood.

Arches

Arches are one of the simplest and most effective tools in garden design. Whether improvised or meticulously constructed, they act as focal points and frames, with an almost magnetic quality that never fails to attract attention.

1 Marion Jay has combined *Rosa* 'Sander's White Rambler' with *Clematis* 'Kermesina' and *C.* 'Princess Diana', to create a delightful, romantic arch worthy of any country garden.

2 Rustic arches have a certain charm and are particularly suited to woodland or shady gardens, as in Kathy Fries' garden in Seattle. Constructed out of branches and twigs nailed together, they are temporary structures that can be easily replaced.

3 Solid frames and arches, like this opening in a granite wall in June Blake's garden in County Wicklow, can be enticing. As architectural elements, they contrast with the soft contours of the planting. Stone arches were distinctive features of historic Italianate gardens.

4 Arches seemingly carved out of hedges never fail to catch the eye. In Rosemary Alexander's garden, the height of the arch is exaggerated but the overall appearance has been toned down, thanks to the simple timber gate.

5. Some of the simplest arches are the most effective. This metal arch, supporting hops (*Humulus lupulus* 'Aureus'), frames the view of Furzelea cottage garden, Essex.

6 Like a triumphal arch in ancient Rome, this Purbeck stone arch in a garden designed for the Chelsea Flower Show by Andy Sturgeon makes a strong statement. Combined with the bench, it emphasizes the perspective and acts as a frame to the garden beyond.

7 Newel-like timber posts supporting single metal hoops make for interesting arches over a patio. While this design by Christopher Masson would be just as fitting in a formal garden, the choice of planting lends it a tropical flair.

Leafy Tunnels

In warm countries, where the provision of shade is paramount, green tunnels offer a welcome escape from the sun. Whether built or planted, they also make strong garden features, defining and enclosing a space.

Green tunnels, created by training and pruning hornbeams or lime trees into shape over a simple timber support, were an essential component of Dutch gardens in the 16th century. In early 20th-century rose gardens, such as Roseraie de l'Haÿ, just outside Paris, the progression of arches forms a long, impressive rose tunnel, displaying climbers and ramblers to their best advantage, while acting as a division.

1 Quick-growing annual plants like sweet peas, runner beans, cucumbers, and ornamental gourds, shown here at Helmingham Hall, Suffolk, can form attractive and functional tunnels in kitchen gardens. They utilize the space well, increasing the yield, while also acting as an architectural feature.

2 Fruit trees such as apples or pears lend themselves to being trained into particular shapes. Single-stem cordons can be trained over supports, as here in West Dean Gardens, West Sussex, until they form a tunnel. Apple tunnels make attractive features in both English country gardens and French potagers.

3 Even in winter, covered in snow, tunnels have a special structural quality. They can be used as corridors, as in this garden by Caroline Holmes, to link the house to the garden or to frame a view.

4 Willow tunnels, as shown here at Bedfield Hall, Suffolk, can be created simply by pushing willow twigs into the ground. They are a great favourite with children, and work best in informal, naturalistic, or park-like gardens.

5 Of all the floral tunnels in gardens, this one at Barnsley House, Gloucestershire, has been copied the most. A custom-made frame of laburnum (*L.* × *watereri* 'Vossii'), planted alongside wisteria, provides architectural interest and floral opulence.

SHAPING THE GARDEN

Creating undulations where there are none, reconfiguring the topography, and sculpting the landscape are a skill and a science, and perhaps the most exciting aspects of landscape architecture. Some of the greatest man-made landscapes and gardens have been created by earth-moving and are lasting memorials to visionary designers. Evaluating the impact and appreciating how forms will settle are vital parts of the design process.

1 The strong sculptural quality of this garden landscape has a seductive beauty. A masterful composition of water, trees, and grass by Charles Jencks has created a unique sense of place.

2 Contouring slopes can define a garden, creating spaces that protect and enclose.

3 Like amphitheatres, grass terraces are something to be admired, as here at Dartington Hall, Devon, where the oversized steps have a sculptural quality. At the open-air Minack Theatre, Cornwall, turf covers the narrow terraces that have been carved out of the cliff and used for seating.

4 Making a garden on a steep slope is a seemingly impossible task but it can produce spectacular gardens, as at St Michael's Mount in Cornwall.

5 This viewing platform in a garden designed by Christopher Bradley-Hole is reminiscent of a Mayan temple. Using landforms to highlight an area, hide an unsightly object, or even swallow up rubble and rubbish has been used in gardens and parks all over the world. The Olympic Park in Munich was built with rubble from the Second World War, creating hills in an otherwise flat landscape.

1

Mounds, Slopes, and Undulations

The difference between land art and natural undulations lies in the contouring. Emulating natural topography takes skill and practice; the contours and the sweep of a slope at its base must be just right, fine-tuned by raking and critically judged from a distance. Land art, on the other hand, must be recognizable as such: bold, even exaggerated, but, above all, appropriate to its setting.

Mounds are used increasingly as noise barriers and visual shields along major roads and railway lines. Planted with native trees and shrubs, these dyke-like structures have become a feature of new housing developments on the fringes of towns in continental Europe.

1 Burial mounds are part of the Neolithic landscape. Here, Alison Wear has used them as inspiration to create a series of grass mounds that are architectural statements and add a sense of mystery to the garden.

2 Dramatic landforms should be allowed to shine and not be cluttered or hidden. In the spectacular Garden of Cosmic Speculation, Dumfries, by landscape architect Charles Jencks, earth has been modelled and built up like giant sand sculptures, layer by layer, to produce amazing shapes. Narrow flowing terraces seem to have been brushed onto the slopes, wrapping themselves around the peaked ridge on the aptly named "Snake and Snail Mound". Landforms like this only work on a grand scale, where they form a cohesive entity that can be admired and appreciated from a distance.

3 "The bolder the forms, the simpler the surroundings" is a maxim that Brita von Schoenaich has perfected in this garden. Peaks and sharp landforms settle over time, so if they are to remain distinctive, each layer must be compacted during construction. It is also advisable to wait until the form has settled before adding the final layer of topsoil and grass.

4

Gardening on a Slope

Some of the most exciting gardens have been carved out of slopes. Villa d'Este in Tivoli, Italy, Harold Peto's garden at Iford Manor, near Bath, and Tresco Abbey Garden on the Isles of Scilly, to name but a few, take advantage of differences in height to create spectacular views, vistas, and microclimates for tender plants.

Terraces are an integral part of the Mediterranean landscape and have inspired designers throughout the years. Gardening on slopes can be daunting but it does provide the opportunity to create staggered gardens, with different areas for a variety of functions. Retaining walls are, however, built structures and should always be properly designed and constructed by professionals out of durable materials.

1 Reminiscent of vineyards along the Rhine, this steep slope in Luxembourg has been mastered with a series of narrow terraces. Irises such as 'After Dark', as well as *Allium stipitatum* 'White Giant' and *Eremurus*, thrive and provide a soft foil to the geometry of the natural stone retaining walls.

2 *Heuchera*, roses, geraniums, and gypsophila are packed into long, narrow flowerbeds in this garden from the Gardens of Gothenburg Festival. The length of the bed is emphasized by the horizontal slats of the bench.

3 In larger country or suburban gardens, where the gradient of a slope is not so extreme, a more naturalistic approach can be adopted. This flight of basalt block steps, which is designed by Peter Berg, leads to the upper level of the garden. The earth has been retained on one side by a modernist concrete wall and on the other by large boulders.

4 The trend for digging out basements in towns and cities is reshaping gardens, creating new challenges for owners and designers alike. Ingenious yet simple solutions are called for. Here, Modular have gently bridged the height difference, clothing each level in greenery, and have incorporated a timber slatted bench into the retaining wall, making the most of the different levels.

Terraces and Retaining Walls

Few gardens are flat, which means that optimizing levels and making the best out of a disadvantage is a reality of modern gardening. Building plots are often in challenging locations, and many home owners are compelled to extend downwards to increase their living space. Split-level gardens are now not only found in mountainous or vine-growing regions but in inner cities, too.

Terraces and retaining walls are unavoidable in such situations. The question is, how many of them should there be and how high? Single, low retaining walls could possibly be built in situ, but anything over 1m (3ft) high has to be designed and approved by a structural engineer. In all cases, retaining walls must be structurally sound as well as aesthetically pleasing.

1 Inspired perhaps by the basalt columns of the Giant's Causeway in County Antrim, this low retaining wall in France is imaginative but also functional. Joints between the stones act as weep holes, preventing a build-up of water behind the wall, which is often a cause of instability.

2 Soaring, high retaining walls are not what most garden owners want to look at. They are not only dominating and dull but also costly. Where there is sufficient space, staggering the height difference can add interest. Timber shuttered concrete walls, as in this Californian garden designed by Shades of Green, have an interesting texture, which looks particularly good in Mediterranean climates.

3 Vineyards and *limonaia*, the terraces on which citrus fruits were traditionally grown in northern Italy, can be a source of ideas for garden designs. Here, an olive grove has been given an air of sophistication by Claire Mee Designs. The retaining walls of the terraces are made of breeze blocks (cinder blocks) and rendered – a practical solution when costs and skilled labour are an issue – with the coping stones adding a touch of elegance.

4 Gabions stacked one above the other are an excellent means of retaining slopes. Here, the rows taper off and seem to disappear into the meadow, in keeping with the natural look of the LDA landscape design.

GREENERY AND FLOWERS

IN SEARCH OF PERFECT PLANTING

Trees, shrubs, perennials, grasses, and bulbs are all part of the intricate framework that makes up a garden. They can create an atmosphere, define a style, be a highlight, or just a backdrop. Some plants are soloists, while others are better in small groups. Learning what grows where and with what is fundamental.

1 There is more to plants than flowers; foliage, fruit, and habit can all play a role. The pocket handkerchief tree (*Davidia involucrata*) is renowned for its exceptional flowers, but the walnut-like fruit is equally attractive.

2 Dogwoods, such as this *Cornus* 'Ormonde', are spectacular when in full flower. The genus *Cornus* ranges from showy varieties and cultivars to subtle European natives like *C. sanguinea* and *C. mas*.

3 The spectacular autumn colour of trees like *Prunus sargentii*, shown here with bright yellow *Cercidiphyllum japonicum*, is bewitching.

4 Nature's art: the attractive, textured bark of Santa Cruz Island ironwood (*Lyonothamnus floribundus* subsp. *aspleniifolius*).

5 Against the orange wall, the fluorescent quality of the seed pods of the snowdrop tree (*Halesia carolina*) seems more pronounced.

6 In this garden designed by Christopher Bradley-Hole, multi-stemmed shrubs, such as *Amelanchier lamarckii*, have their own aesthetic, which is set off by a ground cover planting of *Euphorbia amygdaloides* 'Purpurea', *Euphorbia* × *martini*, and *Anemanthele lessoniana*.

Trees: Scene Stealers and Quiet Highlights

Some trees are predestined to have a starring role in a design, and they need space in which to shine and a fitting backdrop. Other trees may be better in groups, where their position and relationship to each other are governed by the design style. Planted in double rows, trees form an avenue; in a square, with a single tree in the middle, they create a quincunx, a popular device in the 16th century. Positioned in loose triangles, they make a relaxed group, and en masse, a wood or an orchard. Habit and shape are other determining factors that can underpin a design.

1 The Judas tree (*Cercis siliquastrum*) flowers before the leaves appear. Shown here at the Hermannshof botanical gardens in Germany, it is enhanced by an underplanting of *Tulipa* 'Parade'.

2 *Acer palmatum* 'Osakazuki' grows to 4–6m (13–19½ft) in height and prefers moist, slightly acidic soil. It is one of a number of Japanese maples noted for spectacular autumn colour. Here, the tree has been given a more formal appearance by the low box hedging in a garden designed by Jill Billington.

3 Dogwood (*Cornus florida*), growing here next to a house in Connecticut, New England, has an open habit and, like all dogwoods, glorious autumn foliage.

4 *Acer palmatum* 'Atropurpureum' is another of the Japanese maples in this woodland setting at Westonbirt Arboretum, Gloucestershire.

5 Pin oak (*Quercus palustris*) is one of nature's quiet highlights. A medium-sized to large tree that can tolerate waterlogged soils, it is often planted in groups, as in this design by Chris Ghyselen, where the slender, conical crown and autumn colour have been set off by a carpet of *Persicaria amplexicaulis* 'Firedance'.

6 Large mature trees have a certain majesty about them. They also have an undeniable sculptural quality. In this contemporary garden by Arterra Landscape Architects, a valley oak (*Quercus lobata*), endemic to California, is a focal point but also a dramatic backdrop to the seating area.

Bark at Its Best

Buying a tree just for the beauty of its bark might seem strange but in climates where winter seems to last for ever, or at least for five months, it has a particular attraction. It literally brightens up the garden and provides interest at a time when grey predominates. There is, however, an art to incorporating such striking features into a design.

1 It is not just how trees are positioned but what they are paired with that makes a successful design. In the East Ruston Old Vicarage, Norfolk, the serpentine grass path cuts through the wood, transforming the stand of birches (*Betula utilis* var. *jacquemontii* 'Grayswood Ghost') into an avenue. Low ground cover and a muted background emphasize the white stems, a tactic that works for all spectacular bark.

2 The russet, almost orange, bark of *Luma apiculata* brightens up woodland gardens on acidic soil. The small, white-flowering tree grows naturally in the shade of larger trees but is not frost-hardy.

3 Papery, peeling bark is a characteristic of birches and is particularly prominent in Chinese red birch (*Betula albosinensis*).

4 Acers come in an array of species and cultivars, many of them with distinctively coloured bark, such as this *Acer palmatum* 'Sango-kaku'.

5 Striated or snake-like bark is a feature of some maples, such as this *Acer pictum*.

6 Pinky-coppery horizontal stripes make a strong statement, working best in groups, as shown with these birches (*Betula albosinensis* var. *septentrionalis*). Their small, green leaves turn yellow in autumn.

7 The beautiful reddy-brown bark of *Acer triflorum*, a bushy tree that grows up to 12m (39ft) high.

8 The distinct deep fissures of sweet chestnut (*Castanea sativa*) wind themselves like a corkscrew around the trunk.

9 The ultimate camouflage bark: *Eucalyptus pauciflora* subsp. *niphophila*.

10

10 Piet Ouldof's planting scheme on The High Line gardens in New York draws on the natural beauty of vegetation. Here, Japanese pussy willow (*Salix chaenomeloides*) is outlined against the aptly named *Cornus sanguinea* 'Midwinter Fire'. The planting has a contemporary, naturalistic feel, yet the same species in a different setting and combination would create a totally different effect.

11 By the mere fact of their slender habit, size, and tolerance to a wide range of conditions, birches are popular trees for urban settings. They have shallow root systems, thin, delicate branches, and are tolerant of light shade. In the 1960s, landscape architects used them as specimen trees in planting schemes for housing estates (in stark contrast to the mini-woodlands, evocative of the Russian plains, planted today). Notable examples of birch tree plantings include the grove surrounding the Blue Steps in the modernist Fletcher Steele garden at Naumkeag, Massachusetts, and Helen Dillon's front garden in Dublin, which she has transformed by planting no fewer than 51 *Betula utilis* 'Fascination'. *Betula utilis* var. *jacquemontii* is one of the most popular birches. In this photograph, they have been planted close together in the Winter Walk at Anglesey Abbey, Cambridgeshire, to form a thicket with a Hockney-esque quality. As birch is fast-growing, a woodland planting like this will have to be thinned in a few years' time. Such monocultures can be statement pieces but they must be carefully positioned and accessorized if they are to have lasting value in a garden.

12 Winter can be an exciting time in the garden. Careful thought has been given to this planting at Glen Chantry, Essex, which would look good on the fringes of a medium-sized garden. The birches form strong vertical lines that are set off by a fiery backdrop of *Cornus sanguinea* behind *Salix alba* 'Sibirica', to the left, and *Salix alba* var. *vitellina* 'Britzensis', to the right. A carpet of snowdrops picks up on the white of the bark, making for a beautiful composition.

Woodland and Orchards

Trees are an integral part of country gardens. Existing trees can provide the framework for a garden, be a part of the surroundings, or, as in the case of woodland, be the garden itself. In these bigger gardens, the choice of trees is not as limited as it is in urban situations. As long as they are suitable for the location, medium-sized and even large trees can be considered for new planting schemes. Native trees are a joy and will enrich a garden. Not only are they of environmental benefit but they will also leave a valuable legacy for future generations.

Orchards are an important feature of the countryside in many areas, but countless traditional orchards have been grubbed up to make way for buildings. Efforts are now being made, though, to ensure that this landscape heritage does not disappear completely. An orchard could form the transition from an ornamental garden to the countryside, or a low-maintenance option for an extensive plot. Mini orchards of just four trees lend a rural touch to a suburban garden.

1 Broad-leaved woodland gardens have a singular beauty. Spring is a particularly special time when the canopies are open and the light can reach the woodland floor, promoting the growth of a rich tapestry of geophytes, grasses, and perennials. Here, at Tuin 't Hofje, in the Netherlands, the natural flora has been enhanced with tulips. Once the canopy fills, the light is reduced and the mood changes.

2 An orchard in full blossom, whether almonds, apples, pears, or cherries, is a sight to behold. Half-standards, like the cherry trees shown here, have a bushy habit, while standard trees have taller stems and a higher canopy.

3 Pear trees line the sides of a wide garden path in the country estate of Filoli, California, to create a tight avenue. For a more formal, grander look, lime trees, such as *Tilia cordata* 'Greenspire', could be used instead. When designing avenues, the general guide to follow is the larger the tree, the wider the distance between rows and each individual tree.

Small Trees/ Large Shrubs

The search for the ideal small tree for urban gardens has thrown up some inventive and imaginative solutions. Tree nurseries are keen to fuel the demand and, through judicious cultivation and training, they have succeeded in producing large shrubs with the appearance of small trees.

Recent trends have seen demand soar for picturesque shapes and umbrella-like canopies. Useful showcase species available as multi-stemmed specimens include common alder (*Alnus glutinosa*), for watersides and heavy clay, hornbeam (*Carpinus betulus*), hazel (*Corylus avellana*), and crab apples such as *Malus* 'Evereste'. Smaller species, 3–5m (10–16½ft) tall, include evergreen *Viburnum rhytidophyllum*, sumac (*Rhus typhina* – see page 38), and some of the larger rhododendrons, although the last might be difficult to find and expensive to buy. Plants that fit into the small tree category by virtue of their clear stems and the height they reach in warm and humid climates include tree ferns and cordylines.

1 Specially trained high-stemmed Juneberry, or snowy mespilus (*Amelanchier lamarckii*), with their umbrella-shaped canopies, have been planted as a small avenue along the border of this town garden designed by del Buono Gazerwitz Landscape Architecture. Backed by a hornbeam hedge and flanked by box rectangles, the trees appear to be larger than they are.

2 Multi-stemmed amelanchiers have been planted to form a shady canopy. The heights of both the canopy and the fence have been cleverly judged in order to filter out views beyond the boundary. For instant gardens, semi-mature trees can be found at good nurseries. These trees transplant well, are frost- and wind-tolerant, and are suited to urban sites, which explains their widespread use.

3 The attraction of *Amelanchier lamarckii* lies in the flowers, blue-black edible fruit, and glorious autumn colour and shape. Just by changing the type of ground cover, Christopher Bradley-Hole has created an entirely different style from that shown in photograph 1.

4 Dwarf elm (*Ulmus* × *hollandica* 'Jacqueline Hillier') is a slow-growing shrub that develops over time into a rounded crown with twisted branches. It will grow in light shade and forms a dense canopy in summer.

5 Common elderberry (*Sambucus nigra*) is a useful, fast-growing deciduous plant that is native to many parts of Europe. If left to develop, it can form small trees of bushy habit that are almost as wide as they are tall. It is one of the easiest plants to cultivate, as twigs stuck in the ground quickly root. Elderberry is a plant of the countryside, adding a rural flair to the garden with its fragrant flowers and dark blue fruits. Here, it has been planted on the other side of the wall as a screen, forming a transition between the country garden and the fields beyond.

6 Golden rain tree (*Laburnum* × *watereri* 'Vossii'), here with *Allium aflatunense*, is spectacular in flower. Concerns about the poisonous seeds contained in its long pods have led to a decline in its use in gardens. In terms of size, soil tolerance, and ornamental value, it ticks all the boxes, but it must be used with care.

7 Mop-head acacia (*Robinia pseudoacacia* 'Umbraculifera'), shown here in a garden designed by Sue Townsend, is the ultimate "lollipop" tree and ideal for formal gardens. In order to maintain the tight spherical crown, light pruning is essential. Heavy snow should be brushed off immediately, as the weight can cause the canopy to flatten. Other small spherical crowned trees include *Acer platanoides* 'Globosum' and also willows (*Salix alba* 'Hutchinson's Yellow' and *S. alba* var. *vitellina* 'Britzensis'), which can be pollarded annually to form a bushy mop.

8 In most situations, trees and larger shrubs are planted small and left to grow. Here, Fiona Edmond has placed a young smoke tree (*Cotinus coggygria* Purpureus Group), with bright red autumn foliage, in front of dark *Acer palmatum* var. *dissectum* Dissectum Atropurpureum Group. Other small trees with distinctive dark foliage include *Corylus maxima* 'Purpurea', which grows up to 4m (13ft) high, and weeping beech (*Fagus sylvatica* 'Purpurea Pendula'), around 5m (16½ft), with a broad spread.

5

Not-just-for-Christmas Conifers

While yews are widely used in gardens, other conifers have not had a major role to play in contemporary gardens – that is, until recently. Conifers are generally perceived as belonging either in arboretums or mundane 1970s gardens or, at best, as living Christmas trees. But it was not always so. Monkey puzzle trees (*Araucaria araucana*) and free-standing thujas were favourites in Victorian times. They adorn great gardens such as Stourhead, where they are showcased by appropriate planting.

1 Mountain pine (*Pinus mugo*) is native to central and southern Europe. Tolerant of a range of soils and urban conditions, it makes a large shrub or small tree with wide-arching branches and a conical shape. 'Carsten's Wintergold', or 'Winter Gold', with its yellow-green needles, reaches a lower height of 2–3m (6½–10ft).

2 Cedars are impressive trees but generally too big and dominant for all but large, park-like gardens. *Cedrus atlantica* Glauca Group 'Glauca Pendula' is smaller than type, growing to a height of 4–7m (13–23ft), and has a pronounced weeping form. In this garden designed by René Meyers, it is growing alongside box balls in a setting of gravel, lawn, and contemporary seating. The effect is crisp and attractive.

3 *Pinus strobus* 'Umbraculifera', is a miniature version of Weymouth pine. Like other cultivars such as 'Macopin' and 'Radiata', it is low-growing with a spread often equal to its height. Here, it is planted with black, grass-like *Ophipogon planiscapus* 'Nigrescens', which makes its foliage appear lighter and brighter.

4 Crown-lifted *Pinus pinea*, native to Portugal and the Canary Islands, has been planted here by Amédée Turner as a small woodland, symbolic of a Roman arena. The upright installations, built by Friday Harper, pick up the vertical thrust of the trees, adding drama to the garden.

5 Scots pine (*Pinus sylvestris*) is accustomed to growing at high altitudes, so it seems only fitting that Amir Schlezinger should use them in a roof garden.

Designing with Conifers

What all these photographs show is that it is possible to create interesting, vibrant, and dynamic gardens with conifers. It is all a question of mixing and matching, and not presenting them as though they were in a botanic garden.

Good gardens demonstrating a sensitive use of conifers are few and far between, but Alexandre Thomas's neighbouring gardens – Le Jardin Agapanthe and Agapanthe Sud in Normandy, France – combine them with other shrubs in a striking, imaginative way. Here, they are shown in a new light, proving that those conifers we associate with the 1970s can have a place in contemporary gardens. Some species such as the deciduous larch (*Larix decidua* and *L. kaempferi*) deserve to be used more, as does the slow-growing *Microbiota decussata*, a prostrate, cypress-like evergreen conifer, native to Siberia.

1 A tapestry of plants in a variety of shapes, textures, and shades covers the steep slopes of this Massachusetts garden by Ric Ide. Purples and yellows are a perfect foil to the darker, denser greens of the conifers. The alternating rhythm of conical shapes, domes, and spheres gives the garden a relaxed look, belying the expertise that went into its creation.

2 Ornamental grasses are perfect companions for conifers. In Brian and Dawn Dunn's garden, the geometric arrangement of the needles contrasts with the loose, feathery grasses, showing each plant to best advantage. Simple gravel paths wend their way through the meticulously planned planting, which is arranged so that each plant complements the next. Included are *Miscanthus sinensis* 'Kaskade' alongside *Cercis canadensis* 'Forest Pansy' and *Salix* 'Erythroflexuosa', with conifers tucked in between.

3 In this Massachusetts garden by George Cameron Nash, the simple, natural beauty of the pines and the Japanese maple, together with the timber decking, conjures up a feeling of serenity and harmony, with a promise of mountain views.

1

Naturally Slim

Tall, fastigiate trees are hard to ignore – like exclamation marks, they draw attention to a landscape or a garden. Lombardy poplars (*Populus nigra* 'Italica') characterize the French countryside, lining roads and acting as windbreaks between fields. Italian cypresses (*Cupressus sempervirens*) are an integral part of the Tuscan landscape, and when planted in cooler climes, immediately speak of sunshine and warmth. This, together with their space-saving virtues and ability to enhance formal as well as floral gardens, explains why columnar trees continue to be so popular.

1 The long flowers of *Eremurus himalaicus* mimic the shape of the row of *Cupressus sempervirens* behind, diluting any sense of formality in René Meyers's garden.

2 *Cupressus sempervirens* is available in a number of cultivars and varieties, such as *C. sempervirens* var. *pyramidalis*, shown here on the garden island of Mainau, Germany, in among an informal planting of dahlias and salvias, with burnished red *Liquidambar styraciflua* in the background. *Cupressus sempervirens* 'Stricta' is slimmer with upright branches. Like all Italian cypresses, it is sensitive and only moderately frost-tolerant, performing better in warmer climates.

3 Tightly planted columnar trees, each one meticulously clipped, create an unusual feature in this garden. Species that can be treated in this way include *Chamaecyparis lawsoniana* 'Pelt's Blue', *Thuja occidentalis* 'Columna', *T. occidentalis* 'Smaragd', and *T. plicata* 'Excelsa'.

4 Irish yews (*Taxus baccata* 'Fastigiata') have been popular as garden focal points for many years, flanking entrances or lining paths, as here at Tuin 't Hofje, Netherlands. The foliage of *T. baccata* 'Fastigiata Robusta' is a slightly lighter green and holds its shape better, while golden Irish yew (*T. baccata* 'Aureomarginata') provides splashes of colour. These statement trees broaden as they mature and may require wiring to maintain their tight, columnar shape.

Clipped to Perfection

Topiary – the art of shaping trees and shrubs through pruning and clipping – has been practised since Roman times and has become increasingly popular in gardens today. Balls, cubes, and cones, which are the most common shapes, are used widely in gardens of all styles and sizes, and even on balconies. The compact form of box and yew means they can be clipped into virtually any shape, whether geometric or free-form.

1 Cloud pruning – tight clipping to create rounded, undulating forms resembling a dense canopy of trees – is an art in itself. This splendid example in a San Francisco garden adorns the boundary wall. A simpler variation can be achieved using box balls, often in a range of sizes. These are close-planted and clipped to produce a closed, wave-like canopy. The effect is suitable for large and small areas alike.

2 Yew, beech, and hornbeam can be clipped to form columns, which may either be used singly, to frame a view, or be tightly planted on both sides of a path, as in this Luxembourg garden by Nico Hoffmann. The artistic interpretations vary enormously, allowing individual solutions to be created for different styles of gardens.

3 These Asian-inspired, cloud-pruned topiary forms, sold under the name of bonsai, are available in a range of sizes and species, including conifers such as *Juniperus* × *pfitzeriana*, *Pinus contorta*, and *Pinus koraiensis*, pictured here. With their heightened natural form, these statement pieces are best set off by simple ground cover, as Christopher Bradley-Hole has done with *Hakonechloa macra*.

4 Depending on the design, topiary can take on a formal or an informal appearance. Here, common box (*Buxus sempervirens* 'Arborescens'), which is pruned into a variety of shapes, lines a flower border in West Green House, Hampshire.

5 Whimsical figures and shapes, like the yew rabbit and box bird at Denmans, John Brookes's garden in West Sussex, are an integral part of English country gardens.

6 Pleached hedging, best described as hedges on stilts, can be found in historical and contemporary gardens, both in an urban and a rural context. This avenue of hornbeams frames the vista in a country garden by Judith Sharpe. Other specimen trees that can be trained in a box shape on clear stems include lime (*Tilia* × *intermedia* 'Pallida' and *T. platyphyllos*).

CASE STUDY
Shaping the Garden

Balancing the formal with the informal, and the shaped with the natural, to create gardens of a quiet, lasting beauty is the mark of a good garden designer. The Belgian André Van Wassenhove (1934–2002) used topiary in an exemplary manner to design modernist gardens of great style. The beauty of his approach lent itself to individual interpretations – all his gardens are similar but different. Many younger designers have been influenced by his architectural designs, tempered by exuberant planting, but his work is not widely known outside Belgium. Some of his gardens, in and around Bruges, can be visited as part of the Belgian open gardens scheme, *Jardins ouverts de Belgique*.

1 Crisp yew hedges with tapered sides enclose and shape this garden, suggesting rooms within rooms. Perfectly clipped, they have an architectural quality, which contrasts with the large, heart-shaped leaves of the golden Indian bean tree (*Catalpa bignonioides* 'Aurea'), the spherical allium seed heads, and the hydrangeas in the foreground. The hedges flank the view of the conical yew, the shape of which is enhanced by the pastel-coloured hydrangeas in the background. Progression through the garden is gentle and controlled, with paths suggested, not prescribed, which makes the space appear larger. Not being able to see what is behind the hedges, where seating areas are tucked away out of sight, adds to the mystery.

2 Seen from the top of the same garden, the patio is framed by the hedges and the arching branches of the golden Indian bean tree. The simplicity of the design makes for a garden that does not date and is attractive in all seasons.

3 Lengths of clipped box hedging tame and give structure to this otherwise informal garden. Again, contrasting shapes and green tones live at the heart of the scheme. Ornamental grasses and ground cover geraniums can hardly be contained in their bed. Like the dramatic leaves of the umbrella plant (*Darmera peltata*), they take on an anarchic form against the box.

1

Trained Trees

Developed initially to increase fruit production, trained trees have been gentrified and are now being used as space-saving barriers and screens in gardens. These essentially two-dimensional trees can be planted against a wall or can be freestanding. They cast minimal shade and are ideal in small spaces. All espalier forms are based on a clear central stem and side branches in any number of tiers, which are trained in various ways, from cordons to fans, candelabras, and even spirals.

1 In this garden by del Buono Gazerwitz Landscape Architecture, crab apples have been trained on a high, clear stem with a four-tier canopy. Similar to pleached trees but without the rectangular-shaped crown, they create an effective screen. Orange-fruited *Malus* 'Evereste' and red-fruited *M. × robusta* 'Red Sentinel' make most attractive screens, suitable for urban and rural gardens. *Amelanchier lamarckii* and cornelian cherry (*Cornus mas*) are also available as four-tiered espaliers, as is field maple (*Acer campestre*). There are also smaller and more compact versions of espaliered limes (*Tilia × euchlora*) and hornbeam (*Carpinus betulus*), which make taller, more substantial screens.

2 Traditionally planted on the south-facing gable ends of farmhouses, where they utilize the warmth of the building, pear espaliers are a common sight in the villages of central Europe. With age, they take on a picturesque, undisciplined form, which is particularly attractive against the patina of old walls.

3 Tall, clear-stemmed, espalier-trained limes (*Tilia cordata*) with four tiers are used as an architectural element in the De Heerenhof garden, Maastricht. Supported by a circular metal frame, they enclose and define the central bed.

4 The fan shape of this wall-trained row of pear espaliers is undefined when in full leaf, underlining the rural ambience of the garden design by François Valentiny.

5 An impressive established espalier, like this pear (*Pyrus communis* 'Williams' Bon Chrétien'), more than 12 tiers high, can provide the inspiration for a design. By marrying the formal with the informal, Marc Schoellen has created a rural chic design utterly appropriate for the setting.

Parterres and Patterns

Creating patterns on the ground to be admired from above has been used in garden design for centuries. Parterres, literally meaning "on the floor", are the outdoor equivalent of Persian rugs that developed into an art form in the 17th century. Ornate scrolls, arabesques, initials, and more, all meticulously laid in box (*Buxus sempervirens* 'Suffruticosa') edging, adorned the gardens of stately homes throughout Europe.

Ornamental gravel and pulverized brick were used as a ground cover to enhance the patterns, as were bedding plants and bulbs. Simpler versions of these designs filtered through to the gardens of the bourgeoisie and into cottage gardens, where they are still found today.

1 Common box (*Buxus sempervirens*) lines the rectangular beds and the fringes of Rita Streitz's garden in Luxembourg. Box balls adorn the centre of each bed but the sense of formality is diluted in summer by the rest of the planting.

2 Contemporary interpretations of the formal parterre are exciting and varied, often based on mass, rather than linear, patterns. In this design by Christopher Bradley-Hole, cubes and blocks of box are interspersed with meadow-like planting, which underlines the architectural form of the box. Another inspiring modern box parterre is to be found at Parc André Citroën, Paris, where box cubes of varying heights are planted close together.

3 A sense of rhythm and contrasting shapes are the distinguishing elements of this contemporary parterre designed by Penelope Hobhouse. Rectangles seem to have been rolled out on the lawn like oversized rugs. Simply by varying the filling of each section, different effects have been achieved, from the bobbles of the first section in the foreground to the candlewick-bedspread pattern beyond.

4 Instead of sharp-edged hedging, rounded, sausage-like forms enclose and fill this parterre, giving a very unusual, abstract look to this part of Gaard um Titzebierg in Luxembourg. It is neither historical nor modern but very much of its own design and entirely in keeping with the surroundings.

4

Climbers

Climbers are one of nature's survivors, designed to wend their way up and over obstacles, whether natural or man-made, in search of light. They can cover and almost take over their hosting structures: woodland edges seem to drip with old man's beard (*Clematis vitalba*); ivy (*Hedera helix*) quickly conquers ruins and tree trunks; and common honeysuckle (*Lonicera periclymenum*) enlivens hedgerows.

There are climbers that drape, such as clematis; those that creep, like Virginia creeper; those that wind and snake up structures, such as Dutchman's pipe (*Aristolochia*); and ramblers like the 'Kiftsgate' rose. These plants provide valuable height in the garden, and while some might require trellis or wires as support, others are happy to scramble up walls and fences unassisted. Climbers can be dominant or delicate; they can add splashes of colour, like Scottish flame flower (*Tropaeolum speciosum*), which prefers to grow through other plants, such as yew hedges. Other climbers are fragrant, like evergreen *Trachelospermum jasminoides* and honeysuckle, particularly *Lonicera caprifolium*.

1 Unusually well-behaved ivy has been trained to grow in a criss-cross pattern along a wall in San Francisco. A variation on this theme would be garlands hung between posts to form decorative swathes. In both cases, regular pruning is essential to contain the vigorous growth.

2 The suckering shoots of self-clinging Virginia creeper (*Parthenocissus*) in early spring have a graphic quality.

3 Clematis are among the most popular climbers. Their flowers come in a large range of colours and sizes, from delicate *Clematis alpina* to the evergreen species *C. armandii* and showy, large-flowered hybrids such as *C.* 'Vyvyan Pennell' or 'Perle d'Azur', shown here over an arch in Tigger Cullinan's London garden.

4 Wisteria needs support when young but, once established, it can cover whole façades, reaching up to 10m (33ft) in height. This wisteria, with its distinctive violet-blue flowers growing over a pergola, resembles a tree.

5 *Parthenocissus tricuspidata* 'Veitchii', a type of Virginia creeper native to Japan, has completely covered this house. This self-clinging climber and fast-growing shrub, growing up to 2m (6½ft) each year, can reach up to 20m (65½ft) in height. The attraction lies in its leaves, which are a coppery brownish-red when young, turn glossy green in summer, then a wonderful red with tints of orange to burgundy in autumn. Alternatives to 'Veitchii' are 'Green Spring', which has broader leaves, and *P. quinquefolia* var. *engelmannii*, with longer, narrower leaves and slightly slower growth. Other self-clinging species suitable for greening façades are ivy (*Hedera helix*) and climbing hydrangea (*Hydrangea anomala* ssp. *petiolaris*), with white flowers and slower growth in the initial years and suitable for north-facing walls.

6 Roses are among the largest group of climbers and ramblers, with an enormous selection of species, cultivars, and hybrids from which to choose. Ramblers require space in order to flourish – white-flowering 'Rambling Rector', for example, can conquer apple trees, and *Rosa filipes* 'Kiftsgate' can scramble over tree canopies, pushing out long, tentacle-like stems as it goes. Not only are the flowers attractive but the hips are too. 'Malvern Hills' is a David Austin repeat-flowering rambler with small double, yellow-cream blooms and a light fragrance. It grows well against stone buildings, as does the popular 'Paul's Scarlet Climber'. Climbing roses require a growing support. Here, *Rosa* 'Crimson Conquest' is climbing over a brick wall at Bramdean House, Hampshire, with the help of hooks. When selecting climbing roses for a garden design, it helps to consider their style: for example, button-sized noisettes, like 'Blush Noisette', have a delicate, old-fashioned beauty, while the modern climber 'Aloha' and velvet crimson 'Etoile de Hollande' are much showier.

7 White *Wisteria floribunda* 'Alba' appears to be draping itself over this orange wall in a garden designed by Penelope Hobhouse. Wisteria requires support growing against walls, but not on trellises or railings, where the stems twine around in a clockwise direction, with the exception of *W. sinensis*, which twines the other way. Wisteria lends itself to all manner of designs, both in a rural and an urban situation. There are, however, two things to be aware of: their seeds are poisonous, and plants produced from seedlings often take years to flower and are not so profuse.

1

Shrubs: the Second Layer

The days when shrubs were solely planted in gardens to fill gaps are long past. Shrubs are the second layer of planting, an understorey between the tree canopy and the ground-hugging herbs. They can reinforce a design, be a backdrop, a screen, a feature, or provide ground cover. In the design process, deciding where and what types of shrubs to plant comes after the hard surfaces and trees have been determined. Which shrubs are then chosen depends on the flavour of the design.

1 Some shrubs, such as this dogwood (*Cornus sericea* 'Coral Red'), are planted for the colour of their stems. This has been accentuated here by the underplanting of *Libertia peregrinans* and *Crocus vernus* 'Grand Maître'.

2 Elderberry (*Sambucus*), the deciduous large shrub/small tree commonly found in hedgerows and woodland edges, has become increasingly popular over the last few years, thanks to a number of cultivars that have a garden-like quality. American elderberry (*Sambucus nigra* subsp. *canadensis* 'Aurea') has golden-yellow foliage, as does *S. racemosa* 'Plumosa-Aurea' and 'Sutherland Gold'. Both *S. nigra* f. *porphyrophylla* 'Gerda' and 'Eva' have purple foliage with pink flowers, with the latter, shown here in a garden designed by Carine Reckinger-Thill, having the additional attraction of dissected leaves, to give the appearance of a Japanese maple. Feature plants in their own right, elderberry also work well as a backdrop to herbaceous plantings.

3 Tamarisks immediately conjure up a picture of the Mediterranean – these hardy plants tolerate flooding and salt, making them ideal for coastal situations. *Tamarix tetrandra*, shown here, flowers from late spring to early summer, with distinctive, light to dusty pink, plume-like blooms. Other species, such as *T. ramosissima*, flower later in the season.

4 Some shrubs are spectacularly beautiful. *Stachyurus chinensis* is one of the rarer garden plants to grow best on acid, humus-rich soils. A similar, but not quite as dramatic, flowering effect can be seen in the more readily available hazel (*Corylus avellana*).

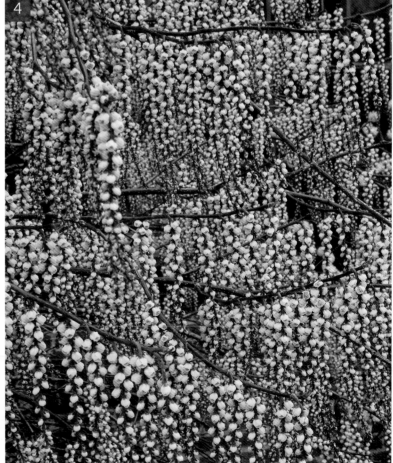

4

Flowering Shrubs

The majority of shrubs in gardens are chosen on account of their showy, decorative flowers. Some go on to have beautiful autumn foliage and berries, too, and attractive winter shapes, while others, such as forsythia, burst into flower, have a brief moment of fame, then fade away to become just another green bush in the garden. Selection, position, and pairing are key to the successful use of shrubs.

1 Hydrangeas – here, *Hydrangea quercifolia* planted against a wall at Greenway, Devon – comprise many species and cultivars, and bloom from early summer to early autumn. The colour of the flowers varies according to the species, from white, cream, and pink to blue-purples. Broadly speaking, the flower heads are cone-shaped (as shown here), spherical, or flat and plate-like, as found generally in the taller, more architectural species, such as *H. aspera* Villosa Group and *H. aspera* subsp. *sargentiana*. These two are also the only hydrangeas that will tolerate chalky soils to some extent. In design terms, hydrangeas are versatile, showy plants, just as suited to woodland or country-type gardens as they are to contemporary schemes.

2 Depending on the weather, witch hazel – here, *Hamamelis mollis* 'Coombe Wood' – can flower from early winter to early spring. These medium- to large-sized shrubs have an attractive habit and a marvellous autumn colour, and work best in a solitary position. The flowers, which are sometimes scented, resemble loose pompoms and range in colour from yellow to orange and red.

3 Mahonia is a shrub that has gone out of fashion and deserves to make a comeback. Low-growing *M. aquifolium* makes good evergreen ground cover, while *M. japonica* Bealei Group works best in small groups or as a specimen plant growing up to 2m (6½ft) high. Both have beautiful yellow flowers, which, like those of *M. × media* 'Winter Sun' shown here, contrast with the glossy foliage.

4 *Kolkwitzia amabilis* is one of a number of flowering garden shrubs, like weigela and deutzia, to flower from late spring to mid-summer. In the garden, they are all very similar in habit, shape, and position to this example at Brickwall Cottage Garden, Kent.

4

Bursting with Colour

The popularity of flowering shrubs changes as trends come and go. Undervalued but versatile lilac (*Syringa*) can be refined or rural, depending on its planting partners. There are over 150 evergreen and deciduous species of viburnum, many of them fragrant, from pompom-like guelder roses (*Viburnum opulus*) to Japanese snowball (*V. plicatum*), with its tiered flowering stems. Both have the additional benefit of autumn colour. While viburnum will grow under the dappled shade of trees, the butterfly bush (*Buddleja*) is best in full sun. Its upright habit is not particularly attractive but the flowers are. Placed at the back of a mixed border, it comes into its own.

1 Some plants are collectors' pieces grown purely for the beauty of their flowers. The Australian fuchsia (*Correa* 'Marian's Marvel') is a case in point. It needs slightly acidic soils and temperatures no less than -5°C (23°F).

2 Weigelas are commonly found in cottage and flower gardens, and can grow up to 3m (10ft) tall. The impressive flowers range from white-pink to crimson. Here, the delicate pink flowers of 'Looymansii Aurea' contrast with the golden-yellow leaves.

3 Rhododendron, from the Greek *rhondon* (rose), and *dendron* (tree), is an apt name for this genus of flowering evergreen and deciduous shrubs, first introduced to European gardens in the mid-19th century. Since then, breeding has produced numerous cultivars, from dwarf to tree-like. All types make dramatic statements, like these azaleas at Boconnoc, Cornwall. Rhododendrons are very specific about their growing conditions, needing moist, acidic, humus-rich soil, with relatively high air humidity and cloud cover, as found in their natural habitat. Such is their beauty and popularity that it is tempting to tweak conditions to suit, but this is not always advisable. They look their best in large groups in shady, woodland conditions, together with magnolias. Although often overlooked, their scent and foliage are also worth considering in a design.

4 At Ramster, Surrey, Japanese maple (*Acer palmatum* 'Atropurpureum') makes a beautiful pairing with semi-double-flowered *Camellia japonica* 'Apollo'. These plants thrive in the same conditions as rhododendrons and also look well planted with shrubs such as *Skimmia* or *Pieris*.

7

Stems, Berries, and Foliage

There is more to shrubs than flowers, which is particularly relevant in small gardens, where there is insufficient space to provide different areas of specific interest. Working with stems, berries, and foliage can do much to enhance a garden at quiet times of the year when there is little other colour.

1 *Euonymus oxyphyllus* 'Waasland', shown here, is similar to the spindle tree (*E. europeaus*) and admired for its spectacular autumn colour and attractive fruit capsules. *Euonymus alatus* 'Compactus' is available in bonsai and umbrella form, for use as a statement shrub in contemporary gardens.

2 The evergreen shrub *Gaultheria mucronata* 'Rosea' grows up to 1.5m (5ft) in height and spread, with distinct pink, poisonous berries that follow white single flowers. A densely branched shrub, it grows best on humus-rich acidic soils.

3 Sloe (*Prunus spinosa*) is one of the unsung heroes of the plant world – a medium- to large-sized shrub with the quality of a flowering cherry when in full bloom. Native to Europe and found in hedgerows, it can have a place in the garden. When underplanted with geraniums or similar ground cover, it takes on a cultivated air.

4 Chinese mountain ash (*Sorbus reducta*) is a dwarf form of the more common mountain ash. Its suckering nature throws up thickets, making it a suitable highlight in naturalistic gardens.

5 Pale-leaf barberry (*Berberis candidula*) is a frost-tolerant evergreen shrub, with yellow flowers and small berries.

6 Stems can have a picturesque quality, like this thicket of *Cornus alba* 'Ruby' stems set against *C. sanguinea* 'Midwinter Fire'. This type of planting works best over large areas, particularly near water.

7 Barberries, like cotoneasters, are very much plants of the 1960s. Then they were used extensively in monocultural municipal planting schemes and gardens but often looked out of place, owing to their distinct upright form and spiny prickles. *Berberis thunbergii* spawned many cultivars, such as the columnar 'Helmond Pillar' shown here. One way to integrate such dominant forms into a planting scheme is to soften them with ornamental grasses.

DEGREES OF SHADE

Shade can be exciting, dynamic, calming, and sublime. Although often perceived as a negative element in a garden, it is anything but. As with all aspects of garden design, successful shady gardens depend on appreciating the different types of shade and how it is cast, as well as a knowledge of the palette of plants that thrive in it. Dappled shade, semi-shade, and full shade are the main categories, each with their own character and charm.

1 The shadows on the lawn cast by birch trees have a strong, graphic, almost theatrical quality; a similar effect is achieved with pergolas. Shadows can be used to enhance designs, especially in winter when the sun is low in the sky and the shadows are longer.

2 Small, enclosed spaces between buildings are difficult to design and plant because they are always in the shade, and they can also be significantly cooler. Using plants that naturally grow in the shade of others, such as this *Acer palmatum* and bamboo, may be a solution, adding interest and colour.

3 Variations in foliage, complementing shapes, and different tones of green are the essential ingredients of a successful semi-shade planting.

4 Some of the most delicate and beautiful spring flowers grow in the shade. Here, in the shade of a tree and a wall, is a carpet of *Cardamine quinquefolia*, *Helleborus × hybridus* 'Onyx Odyssey', and *Primula auricula* 'Blue Denim'.

CASE STUDY

A Shady Garden Par Excellence

Shades of green weave themselves through Emile Becker's exemplary woodland garden in Luxembourg. As with many older gardens overshadowed by trees, the lack of light and competition for nutrients determine what will flourish. Still, these gardens possess their own subtle beauty – they are neither brash nor loud, but quiet and considered.

Gardening on a scale like this takes vision and a certain amount of courage. Recognizing the inherent qualities of deciduous woodland is the first step and enhancing the natural potential the key.

1 The tall, straight tree trunks appear to reach for the sky and punctuate the lush green, semi-shade vegetation covering the woodland floor. The view extends into the distance, interrupted only by the occasional shrub. By keeping the plants low, more air and light seem to penetrate the canopy, giving a generosity of space, which is vital in shady gardens. Ground cover plants, such as various hostas, complement each other well, forming beautiful textural contrasts. Narrow tracks cut paths through the vegetation, disappearing between the large leaves of the foliage only to resurface near a feature or a bench.

2 Knowing where the light falls, where the glades are, and the best position for seating areas and structures is particularly important in a shady garden. In addition to the bespoke greenhouse, there are sculptures scattered throughout this garden, sensitively placed as a reminder of man's influence. Hostas are a key plant here. With textures from smooth to ribbed, and colours and tones from blue-green to yellow-green, they provide variety and are set off by an explosive show of ferns.

3 Spring is always a special time in shady gardens. Erythroniums are a woodland treasure, available in a range of colours, from lilac to pink, as well as yellow. *Erythronium* 'Pagoda' is shown here in the background, with *E. californicum* 'White Beauty' in the foreground.

5

Lighting up the Shade

White flowers, variegated foliage, and glossy leaves are wonderful ways of illuminating a shady garden. Although the flowers might just be passing highlights, they are gorgeous while they last. The secret is to spread the interest around the garden, so that one area after another is in the spotlight.

1 Some plants work in large groups, while others shine on their own. Here, a swathe of hardy perennial, semi-evergreen Caucasian penny-cress (*Pachyphragma macrophyllum*), with large round overlapping leaves, forms a dense cover at the foot of a tree. The white flowers have a sharp scent, which might explain why this useful shade plant is used so infrequently.

2 Variegated leaves attract attention, as do trilliums, so the combination of both is bound to be a highlight. Surrounding tight yellow buds are the dark green-flecked leaves of *Trillium luteum,* which, like all trilliums in their native North American woodlands, thrive on leaf mould. This trillium's variegated leaves are subtler and sit better in the overall composition than those in the cream/white/green spectrum.

3 There is always a temptation to pack in a lot of variegated plants, but if there are too many, they will compete with each other for attention. The most successful approach is to surround a variegated plant with foliage of a similar tonal quality, thus highlighting its pattern, as has been done here. Variegated *Podophyllum versipelle* 'Spotty Dotty', backed by, among other plants, ferns and *Milium effusum* 'Aureum', is the centrepiece of this section of woodland border. Lighting up the front of the border are the button-like flowers of low-growing trilliums.

4 Many more plants can survive in the semi-shade of a light tree canopy. At East Ruston Old Vicarage, Norfolk, a bright and almost brash tapestry of plants – ferns (*Polystichum munitum*) and bulbs (*Narcissus* 'Ice Follies' and *Tulipa* 'Mata Hari'), along with hellebores and clumps of *Acer palmatum* 'Crimson Queen' – adds a vibrant quality to this woodland border.

5 Against the rust-brown branches of *Acer griseum*, the white flowers of *Actaea simplex* 'Mountain Wave' glow like candles at The Garden House, Devon.

1

Shady Greens

Green is so much a part of a garden that it is often taken for granted and almost ignored or, at best, used as background. But it is so much more than that. Green is a secondary colour, a mixture of blue and yellow, and comes in many hues and tones, from matt grey-greens to lush moss-greens and dark, almost purple, green, with many shades in between. Moist, humus-rich woodland gardens and shady borders are opportunities to celebrate this rich diversity and create green tapestries, which, together with the right plants, can be almost self-sufficient once established.

1 Semi-shade planting can take on an exotic flavour, as on this steep slope of a woodland clearing at Haddon Lake House, Isle of Wight. Silver spurflower (*Plectranthus argentatus*), a tender evergreen plant native to Australia, has been planted with ornamental grasses, including *Pennisetum villosum*, and hostas around a waterfall.

2 In the dappled shade of birch trees in Wollerton Old Hall Garden, Shropshire, a wide range of semi-shade-loving ferns and perennials flourish, producing an undulating textured ground cover that is highlighted by individual flowering species, like the white *Corydalis*. Further interest is provided by the variegated plants such as Solomon's seal (*Polygonatum odoratum* var. *plurifolium* 'Variegatum'), tucked away in the corner, and *Aegopodium podagraria* 'Variegatum', next to the path, at the base of the silver birch.

3 Now sadly a garden of the past, Hadspen Gardens, Somerset, was a true inspiration, packed with original ideas. Nori and Sandra Pope understood how to use colour, particularly green, to create different moods. The hosta walk under the shade of high-stemmed hornbeams was a garden in itself, showcasing many hybrids developed by Eric Smith during his tenure at the garden. Here, the spectrum of greens, from matt grey-blue *Hosta* 'Hadspen Blue' to the fresh, nearly apple-green *H.* 'Frances Williams' and white-edged *H.* 'Francee', celebrate green as a colour. Looking down the walk, dark tones increase the depth of the shade, while light tones act as beacons.

5

The Subtle Beauty of Dappled Shade

The current trend for multi-stemmed trees with umbrella-like canopies that cast dappled shade has prompted a rethink in the type of planting that covers the ground beneath them. New gardens, as well as some traditional ones, can provide valuable pointers as to how these shady areas can best be planted.

1 Jimi Blake in County Wicklow, Ireland, is a master of exciting plant combinations, for which he often uses unusual plants. He has perfected the skill of layering and contrasting textures, while retaining a natural, relaxed look. In moist, humus-rich soil, shaded by *Aralia echinocaulis*, a rich tapestry of plants co-exists. Tall, yellow and red candelabra primulas (*Primula florindae* Keillour hybrids) have self-seeded and multiplied over the area and sit well with the vertical fronds of *Dryopteris wallichiana*. The leading plant in this contemporary naturalistic planting is ornamental rhubarb (*Rheum officinale*), with its sculptural, plate-like leaves.

2 In the dappled shade of an old apple tree at Sleightholmedale Lodge, Yorkshire, a carpet of Himalayan blue poppies (*Meconopsis grandis*), pastel-coloured columbines, and *Allium stipitatum* 'Mount Everest', with their tall flower heads, looks almost natural, as if these plants were always meant to be growing together.

3 *Hosta* 'Halcyon', moisture-loving *Rodgersia aesculifolia*, and ferns have virtually swallowed the timber boardwalk through this shaded bog garden in Glen Chantry, Essex.

4 Delicate erythroniums are best grouped so they are not overwhelmed and can be seen to full advantage.

5 This Seattle front garden is a delight. Even though it has been carefully designed and is now managed with the local climate and level of shade always in mind, it retains a naturalistic air. Moss coats the ground, providing a soft, lush green backdrop for the ferns, dark *Ophiopogon planiscapus* 'Nigrescens', delicate *Cyclamen coum*, and star-leaved *Hacquetia epipactis*.

GROUND COVER

How the ground is covered can make or break a design. Some see ground cover as being purely functional, a means of forming a closed surface through which weeds have no chance of growing. Less keen gardeners are likely to choose hard surfaces for the job, while others regard decorative gravel as the ultimate material. However, ground cover is so much more. It is the carpet that underlies the garden, whether as a neutral background or as a feature in its own right.

Graham Stuart Thomas (1909–2003) gave invaluable advice on the topic, which is still valid today, in his 1969 book *Plants for Ground-Cover*. Meanwhile, Professor Richard Hansen (1912–2001) was instrumental in distinguishing between the various plants that make up ground cover. Taking appearance and growth into account, he differentiated between leading, accompanying, and filling plants.

Adopting this concept and sorting plants into groups can help to facilitate the design of planting schemes. The location and size of the area to be planted are vital factors to consider. Lawns and meadows make good ground cover in large open areas, but they are less effective in smaller areas that are in shade, under trees, and in woodland. It is in such situations that perennials, ferns, ornamental grasses, and low-growing shrubs come into play.

1 Depending on the formality of the design both lawns and meadows make good ground cover over large open areas. Here, a hammock suspended between two trees above a long grass meadow lends a gardenesque, but relaxed quality to this Christopher Bradley-Hole design.

2 The fern *Polystichum setiferum* Plumosum Group is used as ground cover under a young *Acer palmatum* 'Osakazuki' in Stuart Craine's design.

3 Sunny open areas in the garden can be just as challenging to carpet with ground cover as shady spots. Here, grass-like *Ophiopogon planiscapus*

'Nigrescens' is scattered between carpet-like lamb's ears (*Stachys byzantina*).

4 Julie Toll has planted drifts of sweet woodruff (*Galium odoratum*), often seen growing in beech woodland, around the base of a beech tree and heightened the effect of the white carpet with clipped box balls and hostas.

1

Monocultures and Mixes

Mass blocks of planting can be dramatic, underpin a design, and have an architectural and contemporary quality. Their use primarily in corporate schemes, though, means there is a general shyness and reluctance to adopt this style of planting in private gardens. However, by carefully considering what is planted alongside and above this lower level of vegetation, the stark monocultural appearance can be softened and complemented.

Tried-and-tested evergreen, compact ground cover growing to a height of 80–100cm (31–39in) includes *Ligustrum vulgare* 'Lodense', *Lonicera nitida* 'Maigrün', and *L. pileata*. Rose of Sharon (*Hypericum calycinum*) was a popular carpet-forming plant of the 1970s and 1980s but has fallen out of favour. However, it does have its qualities. Evergreen, drought-tolerant but only moderately frost-hardy, this yellow-flowering ground cover is suited to urban sites and works well in semi-shade.

1 Ornamental grasses are planted increasingly over large areas. In this scheme by Christopher Bradley-Hole, *Molinia caerulea* subsp. *caerulea* 'Moorhexe', an upright grass with a golden brown, autumnal colour, has been planted with the dark blue threads of *Salvia nemorosa* 'Caradonna', giving a naturalistic impression. In order to achieve such a density, five to seven molinias would have to be planted per square metre (yard).

2 Broad bands of *Hakonechloa macra* flank and arch over the path in this private garden designed by Tom Stuart-Smith. This grass, also available with distinctive yellow stripes in the cultivar 'Aureola', grows well in semi-shade too.

3 Classic ground cover, ivy (*Hedera*) forms a dense mat under the multi-stemmed trees in this show garden designed by Philip Nixon. Ivies are available in many varieties, including variegated forms. Other useful evergreen plants for ground cover include *Pachysandra terminalis* and lesser periwinkle (*Vinca minor*).

4 Compact and clump-forming, big blue lilyturf (*Liriope muscari*) is an evergreen ground cover plant that blends well with other species.

8

5 This bold planting, in a garden designed by Nan Sinton, uses just two species: the dogwood *Cornus kousa* 'Gold Star' and the dwarf, evergreen bamboo *Pleioblastus viridistriatus*, which is a green-striped eye-catcher. Native to Japan, pleioblastus sucker and have to be contained if they are not to spread. They include a number of species that form bushy ground cover and grow in sun as well as shade, such as *Pleioblastus variegatus* 'Fortunei', with its white-striated leaves, and low-growing, dwarf, fern-leaved *P. pygmaeus*.

6 Catmint (*Nepeta*) and cranesbill (*Geranium* 'Johnson's Blue'), here in Ashe Park, Hampshire, form a ground cover that is suitable for sun and light shade. Both die back in winter but are spectacular when in bloom. Cranesbills are one of the largest groups of perennials for the shade, with a variety of species and cultivars, and flowers ranging in colour from white through to dark purple, and all shades in between. The clump-forming, larger-leaved varieties, such as *G. macrorrhizum*, which is partly evergreen, *G.* × *magnificum*, with lilac-blue flowers and good autumn colour, and *G.* 'Johnson's Blue', tend to be best for ground cover.

7 A drift of montbretia (*Crocosmia* × *crocosmiiflora*) thrives here in the semi-shade of Greenway, Agatha Christie's country home in Devon. Often used in woodland planting schemes, particularly in acidic soils, montbretia have a flush of new, light green, spear-shaped growth, which is just as much of an enhancement as the arching orange flowers. The rhizomatous corms colonize areas, often resulting in unplanned ground cover. Woodrush (*Luzula sylvatica*) and such cultivars as 'Tauernpass' make good companions for the montbretia.

8 Such is the pull of snowdrops and hellebores that whole gardens are dedicated to their display. The fascination with these winter-flowering, woodland ground cover plants is easy to understand. Once planted, they virtually take care of themselves, spreading at will and naturally hybridizing to produce flowers of different hues and fullness. Mass planting is particularly pleasing, as proven by this mid-winter display of *Helleborus* × *hybridus* and drifts of snowdrops at Woodpeckers, Warwickshire.

Lawns and Alternatives

Green and velvety, short and perfect, well-kept lawns are the carpet of the garden, the flat, neutral centrepiece that sets off all the other plants. For many, a garden is not a garden without a lawn, but looks belie the care, attention, even devotion that go into their creation and upkeep. They do not just happen, nor can they be left to their own devices. For a more relaxed look, there are a number of ground cover alternatives to grass, such as meadows, which are less demanding in time, energy, and costs, and also reflect different styles of, as well as attitudes to, planting.

Shade, squirrels, badgers, moles, moss, and weeds are all enemies of the lawn. Moss is a natural ground cover in shade and is difficult to combat, and in some cases it is simply best to accept this. A moss covering can in fact be a delight, as many Japanese gardens demonstrate.

1 Lawns are a specialist subject, with specialist firms and groundsmen focused on making and maintaining them. For the lawn enthusiast, there are whole books devoted to the subject, with the older literature often the best. Lawns comprise fine-leaved grasses, such as fescues, which grow to form a dense green sward. Thorough preparation is vital, as is good drainage. As to the question of turf or seed, turf is more expensive but instant. Seed is a science in itself, as not all pre-prepared mixes are suitable for every situation. Neither comes with a guarantee of success, as so much depends on maintenance: a regular cycle of feeding, raking, rolling, and cutting is essential if a lawn like this one is to be achieved.

2 and 3 The clean, mowed edges of this lawn have become a feature set against the row of stone slabs in this garden by Jane Brockbank. The relaxed, almost wild nature of the adjoining meadow emphasizes the precision of the lawn. Mowed in a chequerboard pattern, it has a delightful graphic quality.

4 In a country garden designed by Stevie Nicholson, the organic shape and gentle earth modelling of the lawn promote it to centre stage. Taller ornamental grasses surround the lawn like a frame.

1

Classic Meadows

Meadows are integral to the image of the countryside and alpine areas. The value of these grassland eco-systems has finally been recognized and they are now being introduced into gardens. Naturally occurring grasslands are characterized by a lack of tree growth – the soils are either too thin or the altitude too high, as in the Alps, to support any vegetation other than grasses, herbaceous perennials, biennials, annuals, and geophytes. All meadows have evolved over time, managed by the climate, grazing and, in some instances, fire. Each has its own set of characteristics, from wetland meadows and chalk meadows to the greatest meadows of all, the prairies of North America.

This simplistic definition might help to explain why there is neither one meadow nor one seed mix that suits all situations. Generally speaking, the poorer the soil, the better the meadow. The richer the soil, the more the balance is tilted in favour of the, quite literally, "fatter" grasses, which are great for silage but not for a wide variety of species. It used to be the practice to strip off the top soil and broadcast the meadow seeds on the subsoil. However, meadow planting has developed significantly over the last few years, and new and exciting seed mixes have been developed that take their inspiration from nature but still have a garden-like quality.

1 In a design by Christopher Bradley-Hole, long meadow grasses and a simple mown path through the middle create the perfect picture of a country garden.

2 This mown path in an Irish garden by Dominick Murphy is wider, and the bronze-brown-purple hues are those of a summer meadow waiting to be cut.

3 Whereas grasses are dominant in the two other photographs on this spread – a sign of nutrient-rich, even fertilized soil – here, at Great Dixter, East Sussex, careful meadow management has allowed a rich variety of wild flowers to flourish.

New Meadows

Imaginative interpretations of a variety of grasslands and meadow eco-systems by some talented garden designers, academics, and plantsmen have produced some interesting and inspirational garden designs. They range from annual meadows to meadow-like planting schemes, suitable for large and small gardens and a variety of situations, including roofs and containers. These meadows have redefined the use of traditional ground cover.

1 Noel Kingsbury is an expert in naturalistic planting and the use of ornamental grasses. In his own garden, a drift of *Stipa tenuissima* snakes along the ground, surrounded by a cleverly chosen mix of perennials. In an open site such as this, the elements come into play, with the breeze rippling the arching grasses and the sun's rays heightening the burnished gold of the planting.

2 In a design by Christopher Bradley-Hole, the tall grasses in this understated and tranquil meadow give way to a mown "glade", with a contemporary but rustic timber bench. In the distance, in the semi-shade, the purple tint of the grasses *Calamagrostis × acutiflora* 'Karl Foerster' is spotlit by the sun.

3 Who would have thought that carrots could be so attractive? Wild carrot, also known as Queen Anne's lace (*Daucus carota*), is a European native biennial with umbrella-like, cream to pink-tinged flowers that grows along country lanes and the edges of fields. This meadow at Marchants Hardy Plants, East Sussex, has been seeded, with spectacular results.

4 Set off by sinuous green paths, this meadow in a garden designed by Ian Kitson sits perfectly in the landscape. Oxeye daisies (*Leucanthemum vulgare*), a meadow plant native to Europe, dominate and are highlighted by the reddish tint of sorrel (*Rumex*). There are seed mixes available to create such effects. They should be chosen to suit the soil conditions and do need time to develop.

Naturalizing Bulbs

Long before William Robinson and Gertrude Jekyll promoted naturalizing bulbs in meadows and woodland, William Wordsworth's famous poem praised the beauty of daffodils growing wild in the Lake District. Alpine meadows covered with pheasant's eye (*Narcissus poeticus* var. *recurvus*), and the graceful horned tulip (*Tulipa acuminata*) growing among meadow grasses have never ceased to delight and remain a constant source of inspiration for garden design.

There is, however, a difference between meadow bulbs growing in open grassland and woodland bulbs such as cyclamen. Each is best in a position that replicates its natural environment. Meadow bulbs are their most effective when seen from a distance as splashes or dots of colour. Scattering bulbs on the surface of an established meadow or a grassed area and planting them where they land creates the most natural effect. Calculating quantities can be difficult and depends on whether instant impact or a gradual colonization is desired.

1 *Camassia leichtlinii* subsp. *suksdorfii* Caerulea Group covers this meadow in an impressive show of colour. As camassias flower from mid-spring to early summer, which is later than daffodils, they are often used for a second burst of colour. They also work well in small groups, producing a subtler effect.

2 Snake's-head fritillary (*Fritillaria meleagris*), planted here at the water's edge, which replicates its natural habitat, has been supplemented with white-flowering *F. meleagris* var. *unicolor* subvar. *alba*.

3 Naturalized daffodils, as here in a Tom Stuart-Smith scheme, tend to be dotted throughout a meadow in drifts as the bulbs multiply. Good varieties for naturalizing include the simpler poeticus narcissi like *N.* 'Actaea' , small cupped narcissi such as 'Barrett Browning', and wild trumpet forms like the Tenby daffodil (*N. obvallaris*) and *N. pseudonarcissus lobularis*.

4 *Tulipa sprengeri*, an expensive, late-flowering tulip, has been naturalizing in the garden of Sleightholmedale Lodge, Yorkshire, for over 50 years, to create a marvellously dramatic splash of colour, enhanced by the surrounding meadows. The tulips are carefully managed. After the seed has set, the surrounding ground is sprayed to keep the grass down, reducing the competition for light and nutrients, which allows the tulips to bulk up.

4

CASE STUDY

A Pictorial Delight

Annual meadows have captured the public imagination. The images of the colourful meadows at the Olympic Park, London, which circulated in the press in 2012, did much to promote their beauty.

The vibrant, almost biting, sulphur-yellow rape fields, cornflowers growing among wheat, and *Phacelia tanacetifolia*, used as a green manure, have all inspired a new type of planting. Utilizing the quick-growing attributes of annuals, they produce sensational floral displays that last for a season before fading away. Unlike perennial flower meadows, which demand time and patience, annual meadows are quick to establish and do not require any great gardening skills, other than keeping the area to be sown free from weeds. Many different seed mixes are on the market, with tempting names and even more enticing photographs. As well as *Phacelia tanacetifolia*, mustard, clover, and lupins can also be used as green manures.

1 The University of Sheffield has been at the forefront of meadow design in England. Known as the Sheffield School, it has developed a range of meadow mixtures, including annual seed mixtures sold under the trademark "Pictorial Meadows". Their Candy Annual Mix, used in this design for an English private garden by Colette Charsley, illustrates the diverse species that go into the seed mix to produce rollover colour throughout the summer. Included here are tickseed (*Coreopsis tinctoria*), cornflower (*Centaurea cyanus*), fairy toadflax (*Linaria maroccana*), corn marigold (*Chrysanthemum segetum*), and field poppy (*Papaver rhoeas*). The mix is resown annually in this garden and, because it is a natural product, the results vary slightly from year to year, serving to enrich the garden even more.

2 The annual meadow makes an excellent transition from the lawn to the back shaded areas of the garden, echoing the relaxed country ambience of the design.

3 Vibrant bright colours distinguish this type of ground cover, which can be used over small or large areas, as here, or even on roof gardens – indeed, anywhere with an open sunny aspect or dappled shade.

1

CASE STUDY

Poppy Power

In theory, a wild-flower meadow would have been perfect on the shallow, calcareous soils of this coastal garden in Dorset. But, unbeknown to the owner, the soil had been improved and cultivated over the years. As a consequence, it was richer in humus than the surrounding area and the specially selected seed mix was a spectacular failure. Weeds, not delicate meadow flowers, flourished.

Many would have given up, closed the garden door, and just let the grass grow, but not here. As scraping the top soil off would have been too difficult and costly, an experiment was trialled. The earth was left fallow for a year, the pernicious weeds combated, and seed packets of annual and biennial flowers were broadcast over the surface in the following spring.

1 Field poppies now flourish in the disturbed ground, although some years their showing is not as strong. Never knowing how the seeds, whether collected the previous year or from commerical seed suppliers (including Chiltern Seeds and Thompson & Morgan), will grow is part of the joy and surprise of annual meadows.

2 Here and there, individual foxgloves poke out of the sea of red poppies. In some years, the pastel shades of Iceland poppies (*Papaver nudicaule*) and blue love-in-a-mist (*Nigella damascena*) are stronger, diluting the vibrant reds. Against the green backdrop, this makes a picture worthy of Monet.

3 Grass paths dissect the meadow, leading to the main garden in one direction and a lookout post in the other. The meadow is so glorious that it often trumps the view out to sea. Enclosed on three sides by dry-stone walls and on the fourth by a high, dressed stone wall, it is accessible only through a garden door. A breathtaking secret garden, it is at its best in June.

FLOWER GARDENS

The beauty of a garden in full flower is utterly captivating. There are many styles of flower garden, each with its own specific character. The Victorians were passionate about bedding plants, but their stiff arrangements are no more to our taste today than they were a century ago, when William Robinson rebelled and launched the "English Flower Garden". Romantic and blowsy flower gardens are the most popular today, ranging from the eclectic cottage garden to the tamed prairie garden, and new and exciting styles that combine a little of both.

1 Flower gardens can be any size and shape, with arrangements entirely up to the individual. This elegant country look of orange tulips in tubs hints at the personal taste of the owner.

2 Many books have been written about colour in flowerbeds and how to match and blend the foliage and the flowers to produce stunning compositions such as this. In flower gardening, these types of mixed borders containing shrubs, roses, herbaceous perennials, annuals, and bulbs and corms are among the hardest to achieve, requiring plant knowledge, not to mention artistic, as well as gardening, skills.

3 A loose but powerful, naturalistic effect, reminiscent of a woodland edge or a sunny clearing, has been created by using the strong colours of red-orange *Helenium* 'Moerheim Beauty', yellow mulleins (*Verbascum chaixii*), yellow-green euphorbias, and the occasional white mullein (*V. chaixii* 'Album').

4 The eclectic mix of plants and colours found in cottage gardens, such as in this display at Yews Farm, Somerset, is as much a draw today as it was a century ago, when the beauty of cottage gardens was rediscovered by influential garden designers like Gertrude Jekyll.

1

Painting with Plants

English gardeners are familiar with the name Gertrude Jekyll and her enormous contribution to garden design. Together with the architect Sir Edwin Lutyens, she was instrumental in shaping the look of the English country house and garden. A contemporary of William Robinson, she, too, was inspired by vernacular architecture, romantic village gardens, and roadside wild flowers. An artist by training, with an eye for detail, Jekyll recognized that colours could enhance each other and that light played an important role in how they are perceived. Plants were her palette and with her infinite plant knowledge she composed flower borders of great artistry.

1 Contemporary flower borders owe much to Jekyll's influence. Planting in drifts and staggering plants, with lower-growing species at the front and higher at the back, while retaining a loose, flowing structure, were key features of a Jekyll border. She would have had a clearer colour progression of pastel tones than seen in this contemporary scheme, also featured in photograph 3, which uses colour in a loose and relaxed manner. Red-orange spikes of *Persicaria amplexicaulis* 'Orange Field' are highlighted by pastel shades of *Aster* 'Photograph', with dark purple *Eupatorium maculatum* Atropurpureum Group 'Riesenschirm' towering above.

2 Textures, forms, and colours are used to great effect in this mixed border. Fluffy, dusty pink smoke tree (*Cotinus coggygria*) appears even more delicate against the sharp metallic blues of eryngiums, the large leaves of hydrangeas, and the brightly coloured heleniums.

3 Flower gardens like this are not for small spaces. They need to be able to flow and form a harmonious composition that can be admired from near and afar. Chris Ghyselen has produced a contemporary take on the traditional English border in his own country garden in Belgium. In the autumn light, the fiery colours have a muted glow. Yellow-leaved *Amsonia hubrichtii*, beyond aster-like *Kalimeris incisa* 'Madiva', picks up the tones of tall golden rod (*Solidago*), with red-flowered persicarias leading though the bed to *Miscanthus sinensis* 'Roland', which provides a final flourish at the end of the border. It is not only the planting that sets this border apart but also how the area has been framed.

Cottage and Country Flower Gardens

Country gardens, particularly cottage gardens, have a romantic appeal, and seem to be more a result of happenstance than planning, with plants growing happily side by side in eclectic combinations and often in the smallest spaces. Traditionally, plants for these gardens were rarely bought but grown from seed from the previous year or were the result of a plant exchange with neighbours. Flowers were not merely ornamental but used for herbal remedies and potpourris, and in the kitchen.

The fascination with cottage gardens goes back to the Arts & Crafts movement, when they were perceived to embody country life and traditional values. Cottages cloaked in roses might have looked picturesque from the outside but they were anything but inside. These squalid hovels of the past have now been transformed into gentrified retreats, adorned with flower gardens that captivate the imagination and inspire.

1 Country gardens are currently one of the most popular types of garden. The many magazines devoted to celebrating country life are keen to show contemporary interpretations of the style, like this design by Catherine Janson. It feels wonderfully carefree, with its mix of old and new. A brick pizza oven, reminiscent of an old bakehouse, has a Byzantine quality to it. There is a structure to this garden but it is almost invisible, enveloped by the profusion of plants.

2 Lilies (*Lilium regale*) and roses (*Rosa* × *odorata* 'Mutabilis') appear as if they are growing by chance among the rosemary. It is this casual look that characterizes country flower gardens, where roses are essential ingredients.

3 A cottage is incomplete without a rose draping itself around the front door or over the façade. This chocolate-box image of the English cottage garden has defined the English flower garden abroad, and its charm captures all generations. Among the roses surrounding the window are *Rosa* Iceberg and *R*. 'Charles', with Turkish sage (*Phlomis russeliana*) in the foreground.

4 Flowers and vegetables co-exist happily in this cottage garden, where the flowers of the runner beans are treasured as much as other flowers.

A Traditional Cottage Garden

There are no design rules in cottage gardens, only good, traditional gardening methods involving muck and growing what pleases. Margaret and Peter Hargreaves have been gardening at Grafton Cottage, Staffordshire, since the 1970s. During this time, the number of vegetables has gradually decreased, as more and more flowers have taken over. In true cottage-garden style, there is an extraordinary mix of plants growing cheek by jowl. Some have been recommended by plantsmen, while Margaret has propagated the more unusual ones in the greenhouse, which overflows with plants.

1 All tints and shades of pink, purple, and mauve fight for attention in this exuberant cottage-garden border next to the front gate. Vivid *Astilbe chinensis* var. *taquetii* 'Superba', bought from Eastgrove Cottage Garden Nursery, Worcestershire, seems to be trying to catch up with the hollyhocks at the back. Further forward are *Penstemon* 'Hidcote Pink' and easy-to-grow *Salvia viridis* var. *comata*, with *Diascia personata* to the right. *Sanguisorba obtusa* is wedged in between, while *Lythrum salicaria* 'Lady Sackville' and shocking pink *Silene armeria* 'Electra' are in the foreground.

2 Typical of cottage gardens, every bit of space, including the rustic fence and arch, has been conquered by plants. To the left is *Clematis* 'Hendryetta', with nodding bell-shaped flowers, and *Rosa* 'Karlsruhe' to the right. Lilies are a favourite in this garden. *Lilium* 'Bellsong' is poking out above the astilbes, with the tight buds of *L.* Pink Perfection Group in front. These lilies do not always come true to colour if grown from bulbs, and Margaret is quite ruthless about removing rogue shades.

3 The plants seem taller than usual in this densely packed garden. Bright *Phlox* 'Starfire' picks up the tonal quality of *Monarda* 'Balance' on the other side of the bed, in between yellow-flowered *Ligularia dentata* 'Desdemona' and 'Britt Marie Crawford'. The latter, recommended to Margaret for its outstanding foliage, competes with the lilies for attention. Tall *Lilium* African Queen Group stands proud of the rest, its colour even more vibrant against the dark foliage of the shrubs and purple thalictrums in the background

A Passion for Roses

Rose gardens have changed considerably since the days they were predominantly formal displays of Hybrid Teas. Whereas the emphasis used to be purely on the blooms, today the leaves and hips are also valued. Gertrude Jekyll pioneered new ways of displaying roses, integrating them into mixed borders, and created rose gardens where peonies and lilies were planted alongside Hybrid Teas, such as 'Madame Caroline Testout'. However, the biggest change in rose-garden design was the introduction of English roses by David Austin in the 1970s. These repeat-flowering roses, crosses between Old Roses, Modern Hybrid Teas, and Floribundas, come in a range of pastel hues, from pink to apricot, white to yellow, and shades of red. They also have attractive foliage and sit just as well in cottage gardens as they do in contemporary schemes.

1 The garden designer Dominick Murphy has combined red *Rosa* 'Ruby Wedding' with *Persicaria microcephala* 'Red Dragon', *Knautia macedonica*, and *Geum* 'Mrs J. Bradshaw', to produce a vibrant but delightful contemporary ground cover in an old orchard.

2 In a different area of the same garden, white-flowering *Rosa* 'Iceberg' is used as ground cover under the light shade of the young olive trees.

3 Thorns, as seen in this winged thorn rose (*Rosa sericea* subsp. *omeiensis* f. *pteracantha*) can be just as much a feature as the flowers. This rose grows up to 2m (6½ft) high and has small, white flowers and orange hips.

4 A drift of catmint (*Nepeta* 'Six Hills Giant') sets off the stunning English rose *Rosa* 'William Lobb' in this quintessential English rose garden at Wollerton Old Hall, Shropshire. In the background, *Rosa* Gentle Hermione, another English rose, has been paired with catmint and foxgloves. The tonal quality of English roses can be lighter or darker depending on the light or latitude.

5 An inventive partnership of *Rosa* × *odorata* 'Mutabilis' and *Miscanthus sinensis* var. *condensatus* 'Cosmopolitan' gives a contemporary flavour at East Ruston Old Vicarage, Norfolk.

CASE STUDY

A Contemporary Rose Parterre

The traditional, formal, French rose garden has been reinterpreted and updated in René Meyers's 0.10-hectare (¼-acre) garden in Luxembourg. A formal informality, as it were, pervades the front section of the long, narrow space closest to the house. A designer as well as a keen gardener, Meyers has created a very individual but contemporary flower garden around the seating area, enclosed by tall hedges. A good deal of thought has gone into every detail of this garden, where carefully positioned roses have been used as beacons of colour, highlights, and even as a backdrop.

1 The lime-green table and chair seem to be in a secret part of the garden, sheltered by the rose, the hornbeam hedge, and the conifer behind. By merely adding the box ball and the contemporary furniture, this scene has a fresh, modern feel, even though *Rosa* 'La Noblesse' dates back to 1856. This centifolia rose flowers late into the summer with fragrant pink blooms.

2 Looking across the garden towards the secluded seating area, the parterre has a relaxed, country ambience. Three standard *Rosa* 'Diana' rise out of a band of pink-flowering *Spiraea japonica* 'Little Princess'. Seen at this oblique angle, the white blooms of the rose are set off by the dark green matt hedge, a trick that Gertrude Jekyll used when designing her mixed borders with roses. The plants are positioned in such a way as to create tension and harmony in the design.

3 The shape of the parterre is clear from the upper storey of the house. Cor-Ten™ weathered steel border edging and light grey gravel set off the planting. White *Rosa* 'Diane' is sandwiched between rows of lavender at the front of the bed, while a band of delphiniums leads to the standard roses at the back. Tree-like *R.* 'La Noblesse' forms an impressive cascade of pink flowers, set off by the dark green background. By carefully selecting and limiting the number of flowers, Meyers has made each one very precious, proving the maxim that less is definitely more.

CASE STUDY

A Homage to the Prairies

The North American prairies are the inspiration for a new type of flower garden. Drawing on a rich mix of species, designers experiment with combinations of ornamental grasses and perennials to produce dynamic and exuberant schemes, with naturalistic overtones.

This type of planting has been practised in continental Europe for many years, with the Netherlands and Germany leading the way. Karl Foerster (1874–1970) was an early exponent of the style and experimented with perennials and grasses that grew in similar conditions. More recent champions of prairie planting include Piet Oudolf and Noel Kingsbury in Europe, and James van Sweden in the USA, where a number of these marvellous gardens can be found. At Dove Cottage in North Yorkshire, Stephen Rogers has made this exceptional garden on a 0.13-hectare (⅓-acre) north-facing slope.

1 Similar shapes and colours are echoed throughout this planting: in the foreground, arching *Sanguisorba hakusanensis*, with scarlet *Monarda* 'Talud' in front of veronicastrums, and the arching flower spikes of the grass *Hordeum jubatum* in between.

2 Grasses are an important component of this garden. Their elegant flower heads, or plumes, add a subtle beauty to prairie planting. They weave between the herbaceous plants and act as a link and a foil to more dramatic flowers. The palette of plants shown here includes *Angelica gigas* in the background, purple *Agastache* 'Blackadder', the white umbels of *Selinum wallichianum*, echinaceas, and the ornamental grass *Calamagrostis brachytricha* 'Mona'.

3 This close-up of photograph 1 illustrates the distinct architectural flower heads that characterize prairie planting. *Angelica gigas*, an umbelliferous perennial with a distinct, rounded shape, is shown here with the spires of *Agastache* 'Blackadder'.

4 Prairie planting is mood-evoking. Here, the plants blur to form a composition in which individual species are hardly distinguishable. Box balls form an undulating shape that echoes the movement of the planting and also acts as a dividing line with the adjoining area.

1

A Flower Garden for All Seasons

Unlike other types of flower gardens, prairie plantings look good in winter. Grasses and blooms are not cut back or deadheaded in autumn, but left to stand until spring, providing winter decoration. The seed heads and the arching grasses take on a poignant beauty when coated with hoar frost; the grasses are bleached blonde and even the brown, dead leaves are attractive.

Prairie planting does best in a continental climate, where the summers are warm, the winters cold, and spring is short and seems to roll straight into summer. Plants have to be robust to withstand the frosts and the winds, and this is the key to plant selection. The tamed wild look does not happen by chance and belies the complex relationship of species that goes to make up a prairie planting.

1 Mood, form, and colour come together in this garden designed by Chris Ghyselen. Spires of *Persicaria amplexicaulis* seem to rise out of a carpet of white stars of *Kalimeris incisa* 'Madiva'. The pinks and whites then give way to the browns and yellows of daisy-like rudbeckia, a native prairie plant.

2 Burnets play an important role in prairie planting. *Sanguisorba tenuifolia* has arching cream flowers, *S. canadensis* more erect blooms, and *S. officinalis* 'Asiatic Forms' dark red buttons, as shown here against the striking spires of *Veronicastrum virginicum* 'Lavendelturm'.

3 The spherical flowers of globe thistle (*Echinops exaltatus*) appear to be floating above the ground. This effect, combined with the backlit, veil-like screen of *Molinia caerulea* subsp. *arundinacea* 'Transparent', gives this planting at Sussex Prairies, West Sussex, a magical quality that changes subtly through the seasons.

4 Dotted here and there as it would be in its natural habitat, *Echinacea pallida* pokes through the astrantia bed at Dove Cottage, North Yorkshire, in the same way as the towering spikes of foxglove (*Digitalis ferruginea*) and *Atriplex hortensis*. Taking inspiration from nature and refining it lies at the heart of prairie planting, its aim being to create sustainable plant compositions.

CASE STUDY

Sussex Prairies

Creating a garden out of a field is not for the faint-hearted. The dimensions and numbers that come into play would faze most people, but not Pauline and Paul McBride. Paul is a trained horticulturalist who, while in Luxembourg, had the opportunity of working alongside Piet Oudolf. Learning by doing, the McBrides were able to familiarize themselves with Oudolf's style of planting, which is markedly different from that of traditional English gardens.

Inspired by Oudolf's large planting schemes, they decided to create a garden of their own in which they could put the principles of prairie planting into practice. The 2.4-hectare (6-acre) garden of Sussex Prairies, West Sussex, is the result. Planted in 2008 with the help of friends and relations, it is a bold and stunning piece of landscaping. The McBrides were helped in their endeavours by their choice of site: an open expanse of land where the wind blows through, adding movement to the plants.

1 Contrasts in shapes and forms flow through the garden. Daisy-like *Echinacea purpurea* 'Green Edge', with a strong horizontal note, is set against vertical spires of *Liatris spicata* 'Alba'.

2 Echinaceas are once again the stars of the planting. *Echinacea purpurea* 'Rubinglow' rises up between the button-like heads of *Monarda* 'Pawnee', while the blonde plumes of *Stipa gigantea* form a backdrop. Monardas, a feature plant of prairie planting, grow well in Europe but generally less so in the damp English climate. However, this is not a problem in southern England, where dry summers are becoming the norm. Varieties with Native American-sounding names are generally more robust.

3 Distance and horizons are important for large-scale gardens like this, as is having the space to appreciate the bands and layers of colour that entwine and merge to form a glorious show. In the foreground, *Astilbe chinensis* var. *taquetii* 'Purpurlanze', backed by *Monarda* 'Kardinal', *Veronicastrum virginicum* 'Fascination' seed heads, white *Selinum wallichianum*, copper-orange *Helenium* 'Kupferzwerg', and the red spires of *Persicaria polymorpha*, with eupatorium towering over to the left.

The New Country Look

Garden styles are not born; they evolve. This is true for a new garden style – new country – that has slowly crept up on the public. It is relaxed and quirky, and has an almost fearless use of colour. Above all, it puts plants in the spotlight. Textures and shapes are important but, unlike the broad brush strokes of prairie planting, the planting is like delicate needlework, full of nuances and details. These garden are no quick fix; they are gardening at its best, combining artistry, plant knowledge, and curiosity.

1 Inspired by Beth Chatto's gravel garden in Essex, Gill Richardson has transformed the yard adjacent to her Lincolnshire farmhouse into this spectacular garden. Plants appear to erupt from the ground, in a kaleidoscope of colours. Included are the pastel shades of *Papaver rhoeas* Mother of Pearl Group, *Salvia sclarea* var. *turkestanica*, bronze-brown-leaved *Lysimachia ciliata* 'Firecracker', and orange *Eremurus* × *isabellinus* 'Cleopatra'.

2 Jimi Blake is working wonders in his garden on the edges of the Wicklow Mountains, south of Dublin. It is a plantsman's paradise with exceptional plant combinations. There is a New-Age beauty about it and a relaxed ambience, which is also beguiling. The roof of the outdoor oven, resembling a hobbit's burrow, is planted with, among others, *Hordeum jubatum*, thyme, and chives.

3 Tapestry effects and modern but rustic elements characterize this new design style. At Dove Cottage, North Yorkshire, creeping *Acaena inermis* 'Purpurea' is accompanied by the grasses *Panicum virgatum* 'Red Metal' and *Sporobolus heterolepis*. The almost wild look of the planting is toned down by the rustic yet modern Piet Hein Eek chairs.

4 The simple but beautiful backlit reds of *Sanguisorba menziesii* and *Papaver somniferum* are set off by a haze of grasses in Jimi Blake's garden.

5 Helen Dillon's love of experimenting and trying out new plants in her Dublin garden have produced some exceptional plant combinations, such as the bead-like arching stems of phytolaccas combined with allium seed heads. As with the other gardens shown here, it is the individual compositions within the whole design that make this space so exciting.

6

6 June Blake's garden in Ireland has already been described on pages 28–9. Here is another view of it, looking across the plant beds to the seating area in front of the house. A low-hanging larch, propped up by supports, defines this space and enhances the soft, organic shapes of the planting. Whereas in other parts of the garden a complex medley of species goes into making the intricate compositions, plants are repeated in this section. Echoing the box hedge that meanders through the bed, vibrant *Achillea millefolium* 'Cassis' links the foreground to the background with splashes of colour. The allium seed heads are subtler and provide vertical movement to the planting. Green is the main colour, which is not true of many gardens, but it is used to great effect here, with blues such as catmint (*Nepeta racemosa* 'Walker's Low') playing a supporting role.

7 Christopher Bradley-Hole has incorporated the new country look into many of his schemes, to produce gardens with character that draw on the wider landscape. His gardens are often large, as here, and appeal both from a distance and close-up. This well-considered planting includes dark red *Helenium* 'Dunkle Pracht', which is repeated through the bed, patches of *Penstemon* 'Schoenholzeri' and *Campanula lactiflora*, with thalictrum rising up at the back. Grasses bind the intricate planting together – a new take on the traditional English mixed border.

8 Great Dixter in East Sussex is perhaps the spiritual home of new country. This garden has been making, not following, trends for decades. The influence of Christopher Lloyd (1921–2006) on the gardening world is undeniable. In a typical, no-nonsense way, he showed how to be brave, curious, and experimental, famously digging up the rose garden at Great Dixter, to make room for an exotic garden. Fergus Garrett has continued Lloyd's work, developing and experimenting with plant combinations, to produce schemes of a relaxed but intricate beauty. Layered yet soft, species interweave but allow the occasional vertical plant like *Atriplex hortensis* and *Verbena bonariensis* to poke through. Here, red-orange *Lychnis chalcedonica* is in the foreground, next to fuchsia-pink *L. coronaria*, with a tall mound of fluffy white *Persicaria polymorpha* in the middle distance and blonde *Stipa gigantea* dotted here and there.

Next spread Forms and textures are as important as colour in this uncontrived-looking white garden by Tom Stuart-Smith.

CASE STUDY

New Country – in the City

Bringing the country look to the city is not easy. Often it results in a dated pastiche that sits uncomfortably in its surroundings. The garden designer Declan Buckley understands scale and recognizes potential, and he has transformed an ordinary east London garden into a sublime composition. While most urban gardens are shaded, this almost square space is open and sunny, presenting the opportunity to create something quite spectacular.

1 Mixing and layering plants can result in a planting that is bitty and fragmented but here it is both dramatic and soothing. The light touch is achieved with the help of *Miscanthus sinensis* 'Emmanuel Lepage' along the boundary wall, and light purple *Verbena bonariensis* catching the light behind. Although the olive tree is a Mediterranean native, it does not seem incongruous when seen with the rest of the planting: fennel (*Foeniculum vulgare* 'Giant Bronze'), lavender, distinctive *Eryngium giganteum* 'Silver Ghost', and feathery *Stipa lessingiana*. The wall acts as a screen and a full stop, separating this space from what lies beyond and adding a sense of mystery.

2 The lower basement of the house flows seamlessly into the garden, and the dark slate retaining wall appears as a shadow, so that the view extends over the planting. Carefully positioned trees and shrubs filter and frame the garden, distorting proportions so that it appears endless. The carefree style of the planting sits well with the neutral paving and the modern lines of the garden furniture, creating a very individual, contemporary look.

3 Levels are not dramatic in this garden but considered. By spreading the difference in height from the lower-ground floor to the back of the garden, three different interlinking spaces have been created.

4 On the third level, hidden from view by a screen of *Calamintha nepeta* subsp. *nepeta* 'Blue Cloud', a secluded seating area has been created. The low retaining wall of this upper level doubles up as a long bench – one of a number of clever features in this dream-like, enchanting garden.

The Beauty of Bulbs

Bulbs are essential garden ingredients, and spring certainly would not be the same without a show of them. They enrich shady gardens, as they do meadows and flowerbeds. Chosen wisely, they can provide colour all year round: snowdrops in winter, narcissi in spring, eremurus in summer, and crocuses in autumn. Appreciating their natural habitat is useful when deciding where to plant bulbs, as this will give a good indication of how they will fare. There is a wealth of colours and forms to choose from. One of the best places to see bulbs at their most dashing is at the Great Pavilion at the RHS Chelsea Flower Show in London.

1 Pheasant's eye (*Narcissus poeticus* var. *recurvus*), planted here in an orchard, grows naturally in meadows, and flowers later than other narcissi. Like many of the species and cyclamineus narcissi, such as yellow-flowering *N.* 'Peeping Tom', it will naturalize to form carpets of colour.

2 A narrow band of white bulbs with a scattering of yellow viridiflora tulips flows between the box balls in this white garden at De Heerenhof, Maastricht. White late-flowering *Tulipa* 'Casablanca' is scattered among *Narcissus* 'Ice Wings' in a design that could equally be used in a container.

3 Dark, almost black, *Tulipa* 'Queen of Night' and late-flowering, long-stemmed *T.* 'Maureen', with its marble-white blooms, are combined with *Erysimum* 'Bowles's Mauve' and lime-green euphorbia in this contemporary planting scheme.

4 Snowdrops are one of nature's wonders, flowering in winter at a time when everything else appears dead. The common snowdrop (*Galanthus nivalis*) has spawned many cultivars, such as *G. nivalis* f. *pleniflorus* 'Doncaster's Double Charmer', shown here.

5 The Dutch are masters at tulip cultivation and planting, as shown in this garden by Hetty van Baalen. Among the eclectic mix of tulips are pink-striped *Tulipa* 'Flaming Purissima', double white 'Exotic Emperor', purple 'Negrita', and pink 'Rosalie', all growing with forget-me-nots beneath an apple tree. White *Narcissus* 'Thalia' and magenta *Tulipa* 'Abigail' are planted in large baskets.

CASE STUDY

Tulips En Masse

Tulips are by far the most popular of bulbs, with a long and colourful history. There is beauty in a single tulip, but when they are planted en masse, the effect is breathtaking. The tulip fields of Keukenhof in the Netherlands regularly draw thousands of visitors, and few would ever contemplate designing a garden to rival their display. But Philippa Burrough has done just that, albeit on a slightly smaller scale, at Ulting Wick, Essex. She has transformed a rubble-filled farmyard into a glorious garden, with four 6.5 × 4.4m (21 × 14½ft) beds lined with box hedging, and brick paths around a central circular bed. Dahlias reign in summer, but spring is the time for tulips. The extravaganza does not stop in the farmyard; it continues into the woodland garden and along the fringes of the buildings, with thousands of bulbs planted afresh each year.

1 Against the dark boards of the outbuildings, the tulips appear even more vibrant and spectacular. *Narcissus* 'Ice Wings', planted in a copper container, is surrounded by a mixture of fuchsia-pink, triumph *Tulipa* 'Barcelona', together with dark purple 'Queen of Night', and single late, white-flowered 'Maureen'. Philippa regards the tulips as annuals and therefore an opportunity to experiment with new colourful combinations every year.

2 Showy tulips – double, peony-like, pink *Tulipa* 'Angélique'; velvety, deep purple-fringed 'Black Jewel'; and viridiflora 'China Town', pink, streaked with green – are arranged in a narrow border where they can be best admired.

3 Lily-flowered tulips work well with other plants. Here, orange *Tulipa* 'Ballerina' and 'White Triumphator' have been planted alongside delicate 'Spring Green', a less showy, natural-looking viridiflora tulip, all of them harmonizing well with lady's mantle (*Alchemilla mollis*).

4 The pink petals of the open lily-flowered *Tulipa* 'Mariette' appear lighter in the sun and against the deep crimson triumph tulip 'Jan Reus', purple 'Negrita', and opulent 'Abu Hassan', with its terracotta-red, golden-edged petals. It is not only the colours that produce a stunning display, but the shapes too.

Summer Bulbs and Rhizomes

Once the spring bulbs are over, it is time for the summer bulbs, corms, tubers, and rhizomes. Lilies, dahlias, and iris are only a few of the geophytes that enrich the garden. Most prefer open ground and come from a Mediterranean-type climate. Foxtail lily (*Eremurus*) is native to the sunny, rocky hillsides of Central Asia; quamash (*Camassia*) grows on the North American prairies; and alliums are widespread, from native European chives to large, spherical *Allium cristophii* of northern Iran. Many are showcase plants with spectacular flowers.

1 African lilies (*Agapanthus*) are often grown in pots but they are equally stunning in the ground, provided there is little or no frost. They thrive in cramped conditions and warmth. A marvellous combination is lavender with large blooms of *A.* 'Blue Triumphator'. Here, at Marchants Hardy Plants, East Sussex, a more natural look has been achieved with 'Kew White' and 'Blue Moon' growing as a clump on the edge of a meadow.

2 *Nectaroscordum siculum* is tall and elegant, with unusual delicate hanging flowers that develop out of a cocoon-like bud. It flowers from late spring to early summer, and is best set against a dark background. Here, at the Beth Chatto Gardens in Essex, they have been planted against a backdrop of *Genista hispanica*.

3 Tall bearded irises are among the most luxurious-looking flowers. The sword-shaped, upright leaves have an architectural quality. The rhizomes – elongated, swollen, fleshy underground modified stems – often form a mat on the surface, which has been cleverly hidden here by the large leaves of *Cynara cardunculus*. This is a beautiful planting full of textures and shapes, with tall bearded *Iris germanica* 'Blackout' alongside *Allium hollandicum* 'Purple Sensation' and lime-green euphorbias in the background.

4 Depending on the design style, *Allium hollandicum* 'Purple Sensation' can be sophisticated or flamboyant. Planted at Great Dixter with *Papaver commutatum* 'Ladybird' and delicate *Nectaroscordum siculum*, the effect is spectacular. While 'Purple Sensation' flowers from late spring to early summer and works well en masse, other alliums such as *A. cristophii* and *A.* 'Globemaster' are later-flowering, dramatic, and best planted singly or in small groups.

The Exotic Look

Large leaves, overlapping and overhanging evergreen vegetation, and flowers in bold primary colours are all key to the exotic look. The gardener and writer Christopher Lloyd was instrumental in bringing this style to cooler climates, proving that hot colours, lush greens, dramatic leaves, and towering plants could be combined to create voluptuous, striking gardens.

1 The scarlet new spiky growth of *Fascicularia bicolor* subsp. *canaliculata*, a hardy bromeliad, has an otherworldly look to it. Plantswoman Helen Dillon aptly calls it the 'monkey's bottom plant'. In its native habitat, and in some parts of Cornwall, it grows on trees, but in gardens it is normally on the ground, as shown here alongside *Puya chilensis*.

2 In this shady garden designed by Marty Hoffmann, *Acanthus spinosus*, with large glossy leaves and foxglove-like prickly flowers, has been combined with, among other plants, bamboo (*Phyllostachys aureosulcata* f. *spectabilis*) and large-leaved *Macleaya cordata*, to create an exotic look.

3 Ginger lilies (*Hedychium gardnerianum* is pictured here) are flamboyant and so beautiful that garden owners in northern climes are often tempted to grow them outside. This is successful only in very mild winters, and even then the plants need protection. It is better to plant them in pots, overwinter them, and roll them out once the frosts have gone. Scarlet *Lobelia cardinalis* 'Queen Victoria' has the same flamboyant look but is hardy.

4 Cannas have all the attributes of an exotic plant, from the leaves to the blooms. By a stream at Haddon Lake House, Isle of Wight, *Canna* 'Orange Punch' is sandwiched between tree ferns (*Dicksonia antarctica*) and the grass *Pennisetum orientale* 'Tall Tails'. *Canna* 'Musifolia' is a great substitute for banana plants, with large leaves but less showy flowers.

5 Paul and Patsy Harrington are bird-keepers at London Zoo, so it seems natural that they would want to bring the exotic home with them. The city climate is favourable, with its wet winters and warm summers, and by layering and mixing they have achieved the exotic look in a small garden. *Callistemon rigidus* frames the entrance with echiums behind. The picket gate and the dense vegetation in the background underline the Caribbean look.

6 Everything in this garden, from the plants to the table and seat, suggests a warm, humid climate, perhaps Australia, even the North Island of New Zealand, but the location is, in fact, southern England. Plant knowledge and a flair for positioning plants, so that one sets off the next, is the key to this garden designed by John Bailey. From left to right: yellow-stemmed *Phyllostachys bambusoides* 'Castillonii', with glossy leaved *Illicium anisatum* in front; ginger lily (*Hedychium gardnerianum*) rising like flames against a backdrop of the star-shaped, matt leaves of *Rhododendron bureavii*; the fronds of the palm *Cyathea australis* shading the green-purple foliage of the smoke tree (*Cotinus coggygria* 'Royal Purple'); the tree *Eucalyptus gunnii*. The bonsai-looking *Arbutus unedo* f. *rubra* and young *Agave montana* in pots on the table and the 19th-century French seat complete this section of the garden.

7 Elephant ears (*Alocasia macrorrhiza*), a native of Malaysian rainforests, is planted in a barrel container, set on wheels for ease of movement.

8 Lamorran House Gardens in Cornwall, also shown in photograph 9, is a marvellous example of how planting can transport a person to another place. Containing palms such as *Chamaerops humilis* and Chusan palm (*Trachycarpus fortunei*), as well as aloes, the garden could quite easily be on the French Riviera. Its windbreaks and south-facing slopes, which create a microclimate, are essential for the survival of these tender species.

9 Palms provide the backdrop to a bed of succulents, which include rosettes of aeoniums, sword-like agaves, and aloes, thriving among the rocks. Care has been taken in the positioning of each plant so that the effect is naturalistic. The walled Mediterranean garden at Lamorran House is equally inspiring, showing what is possible with enthusiasm, plant knowledge, and experience.

10 Henstead Exotic Garden, Suffolk, also shown on page 276, is an inspiration and a celebration of the beauty of exotic foliage. Viewed through the windows of the summerhouse is a screen of bamboo and wavy, blue-grey pampas grass with upright plumes. Other large-leaved, ornamental plants, like *Ricinus communis*, which also features in this garden, are best planted singly. Weighing up what can overwinter and what has to be brought indoors is vital in northern climes. That said, the possibilities are immense in warmer regions, such as the southwest coast of Britain or the Rhine Valley in Germany.

9

10

VEGETABLES BY DESIGN

Vegetable cultivation is creeping back into gardens. Allotments, once the preserve of elderly gentlemen, are back in vogue. In cities, vegetables and herbs are grown in small containers, on balconies, and in window boxes. Fuelled by an interest in cooking and the benefits of growing your own, many more people are taking up productive gardening. Vegetables are no longer tucked away at the back of the garden, but are valued as much for their beauty as for their harvest. Previously abandoned kitchen gardens are being opened up and replanted.

1 Aesthetics were not high on the agenda in the average pre-war garden; the main concern then was to grow plants that were edible and useful. In cottage gardens, plants such as nasturtiums were valued for the taste of their peppery flowers and leaves, and also for their seeds, which were pickled as a substitute for capers. Nasturtiums also served a vital role in attracting blackfly away from brassicas and beans.

2 There is renewed interested in the ornamental qualities of vegetables. Bunny Guinness has come up with this quirky design that uses painted bamboo canes as a support for cucumber 'Long Green Ridge'. Brightly coloured capsicum 'New Mex Twilight' picks up the purple colour, while the large leaves of chard 'Granda Rossa' contrast well with the rounded cucumber leaves.

3 A row of cabbages planted in a bright orange container has a surprisingly contemporary look.

4 Sweetcorn 'Conqueror' and black radish combine with dahlias (*D*. 'Karma Lagoon' and 'Bishop of Llandaff') in a fresh take on the traditional walled kitchen garden at Haddon Lake House, Isle of Wight.

All in a Row

There is something pleasing about neat rows of vegetables. It is not just the rhythm and the order but the contrasting shapes, from spherical or pointed cabbages to erect sticks of celery to floppy bush beans. The distance between plants and rows is based on practical considerations, so that each plant is allocated enough space to develop free of competition from neighbours. Some gardeners have fine-tuned the art of companion planting, whereby one variety acts as a decoy, luring bugs away from the crops. Alternating rows of chives and carrots, or onions and love-in-the-mist (*Nigella*), is both beneficial and beautiful.

1 Winter might be a quiet time in the vegetable garden, but there are some crops, such as Brussels sprouts, that add interest to it and provide food for the table. Novelty red Brussels sprouts 'Red Bull', which darken as the temperature drops, are shown here alongside normal green sprouts. William Robinson was very particular in how he designed the walled garden here at Gravetye Manor, West Sussex. He wanted a range of growing conditions, from well-draining to slightly damp soil, as well as warm and cool spots, so he laid out the garden on a slope with a surrounding oval wall.

2 Rows need not be straight; they can be concentric, as in these beds at Scampston Hall, North Yorkshire, for an ornamental effect. Cabbages are planted in front of purple curly kale (borecole) 'Redbor', globe artichokes, and 'Nero di Toscana', also known as 'Cavalo Nero' or 'Black Russian.'

3 There are leeks, and there are exhibition leeks. Both 'Yorkshire Green', on the right, and 'Sammy Dickinson Cross', on the left, are pot leeks that used to be grown and exhibited with pride throughout the northeast of England. In this show garden by Gillian van der Meer, Mary Payne, and Jon Wheatley for the 2010 RHS Hampton Court Flower Show, they have been planted alongside blue-stemmed kohlrabi.

4 Lettuces, such as these butterheads, take on an ornamental quality when planted together with red oak-leaved or 'Lollo Rosso' types in a grid system. The onions growing between the rows of lettuce in this kitchen garden at Barnsley House, Gloucestershire, appear like brush stokes.

Perfect Potagers

The French are masters of the art of the potager, which is simply a kitchen garden with ornamental value. In a potager, the utmost care is paid to how the vegetables are displayed – the rows are meticulous and the variety of plants grown astounding. Unlike English walled kitchen gardens, potagers are not separated from the house. At Château de Miromesnil, the potager is next to the house, and at Villandry, it is designed as a geometric pattern to be seen from above. Colour is just as important here, as seen in the rainbow potager of Château du Bosmelet, where Louis Benech and Laurence de Bosmelet have created an exceptional kitchen garden with a contemporary elegance. Domaine Saint-Jean de Beauregard, near Paris, is another inspirational potager. It is full of ideas that can be transferred to much smaller gardens, even allotments.

1 Rosemary Verey (1919–2001) was instrumental in making ornamental vegetable gardens fashionable. She built a potager adjacent to the main garden of Barnsley House in 1979, taking inspiration from *The Country Housewife's Garden* written in 1617 by William Lawson. The almost square plot was divided into beds with narrow brick paths crisscrossing the garden. Low, neatly clipped box hedges surround the beds, the corners are marked with box balls, and the centre of the garden is marked by four columnar Irish yews that seem to rise out of a sea of green. Despite the formal layout, the garden has an informal, very English feel. This is partly due to the flowers like columbine (*Aquilegia*), yellow *Meconopsis cambrica*, and blue forget-me-nots, which grow wherever they choose.

2 At Barnsley House, it is not a question of growing the biggest and the best vegetables, but the most attractive. It takes skill to juggle the wild with the tame and so maintain an English country potager that has been copied the world over.

3 Colourful tulips frame the edge of the raised bed and enclose the cold-frames built out of sheet glass in a kitchen garden designed by Tom Stuart-Smith.

4 Large cabbages, growing in the style of Villandry, encircle the artichokes in this vegetable border.

CASE STUDY

A Kitchen Garden for All Seasons

Every country hotel seems to have its own supply of fresh vegetables, and now that trend has filtered down to private houses. Work on the kitchen garden at Ashe Park, Hampshire, started in autumn 2010, and by the following spring the first vegetables were sown. Laura Hazell had developed a potager at her previous house, taking inspiration from Rosemary Verey (see page 248) and Marylyn Abbott of West Green House, Hampshire, so she knew, as she says, what she liked and what worked. Garden designer Andrew Woolley developed her ideas into reality: an impressive 0.26-hectare (²/₃-acre) sunken kitchen garden that is both productive and decorative.

The basic form is that of a square overlaid with a cross of broad grass paths. Each quarter is subdivided by diagonal paths, but whereas in traditional schemes all the planting beds would be lined with box hedging, here they alternate with raised timber beds. This variation in height, materials, and shapes defines this garden, as does the contrast between the functional and the ornamental.

1 Triangular fruit cages in the far corner of each quarter contrast with elaborate obelisks and rustic yet elegant raised beds. First impressions are of a green and white ensemble. Look closer and the details become apparent: a clump of orange-red flowers among the sweet corn, red-leaved lettuces around chard, and pinpricks of orange marigolds at the foot of the box hedge. Russet Cor-Ten™ weathered steel edging around the box hedge beds reinforces the subtle invasion of colour.

2 Cabbages, red-bronze, oak-leaved lettuces, and onions with marigolds in among them are protected in a wire-mesh cage surrounded by low box hedging. In the raised bed beyond, rows of lettuces and onions accentuate the length of the bed.

3 The extent and overriding formality of the garden are apparent from this angle. A spherical slate water feature marks the centre. However, what sets this garden apart are the sculpted grass banks. Like an amphitheatre, they surround the garden on two sides and are a dramatic transformation from the breeze-block walling that was here originally.

1

Raised Beds and No-Dig Vegetable Gardens

Alongside the classic methods for growing vegetables and fruit, new ways of cultivating food for the table, such as the no-dig method, have been developed. This is ideal for poor soil or difficult conditions: seeds and seedlings are planted in a thick layer of well-rotted manure, topped with a dressing of compost. The nutrient-rich layers improve the existing soil, suppress weeds, encourage worms, and lead to better crops and easier gardening.

1 Raised beds come in all shapes and forms, from traditional timber-enclosed beds to more inventive solutions. These vegetable beds, from a design by Bunny Guinness for the 2011 RHS Chelsea Flower Show, are shown with an integrated bench. The beds are surrounded by woven willow, which is a sustainable product that, depending on the planting, can take on a rustic or contemporary appearance. Flowers and vegetables have been cleverly interplanted to produce unusual combinations of contrasting colours, such as burgundy-stemmed Swiss chard and lime-green *Euphorbia characias* subsp. *characias* 'Humpty Dumpty'.

2 Devised by Patricia Fox, this ingenious combination of tall-growing capsicums and ground-hugging lettuce, growing in a metal container, provides aesthetic interest as well as plentiful cropping.

3 At West Green House, Hampshire, wicker baskets with inset bags, which can be easily removed, make ideal tiny raised beds for small gardens and balconies that are aiming for a rustic look.

4 Continuing the theme of the modern potager and the use of raised beds, this garden by Joakim Seiler for the Gardens of Gothenburg Festival, Sweden, pays homage to the triangular modernist garden of Villa Noailles in Hyères, France. While the lower bed is devoted to green and yellow foliage herbs, such as thyme and sage, the upper bed showcases the burgundy hues of 'Lollo Rosso' lettuce.

9

5 Vegetable gardening can be back-breaking, and raised beds are one way of making it less arduous. They are also an excellent device for cultivating crops on poor soil. Using the no-dig method promoted by the organic gardener Charles Dowding, raised beds can be filled with a layer of rotted farm manure or garden compost, then topped by a finer layer such as mushroom compost, thereby providing a good growing medium. Wider timbers, as used for this bed at Alfriston Clergy House, East Sussex, can double up as an impromptu bench or a useful ledge.

6 It is amazing how much has been packed into this single raised bed. In a balcony design by Claire Mee Designs, Swiss chard, salad leaves, rosemary, and other herbs, as well as a strawberry plant, have been arranged beautifully around the base of three standard olive trees, to create the ultimate small vegetable garden.

7 An old-world atmosphere defines this exceptional ornamental kitchen garden by George Carter. Small enclosed ornamental flower gardens and physic gardens of medicinal herbs date back to medieval times. Known as herbers, they were an important part of the garden, comprising raised square beds and fences of wattle or, later, diamond trellis fences. George Carter has fronted this raised bed with latticework and marked the corners with turned newels. Trelliswork, or treillage, was an important feature of historical gardens up to the baroque period. It was used to erect all manner of structures, like the arbour situated in the top right-hand corner of this photograph.

8 In a garden designed by Claire Mee Designs, the lawn has been transformed into a contemporary kitchen garden by the addition of rhythmically placed raised beds. While vegetables grow in lower beds, espalier apple trees, underplanted with strawberry plants, are in taller, timber plant containers.

9 Raised beds come in any number of shapes and forms. Even recycled metal containers can be used to grow salad leaves, herbs, and even strawberries, opening possibilities for the budding gardeners with no garden but a sunny balcony, roof terrace, or windowsill instead.

CASE STUDY

The Good Life

The garden of the Straw House on Stock Orchard Street in north London is just as surprising as the building. True to the ethos of this design project, the garden is no slick, landscaped space but an essential contribution to sustainable living in the city.

With an eye for the unusual and the ability to design low-impact, contemporary passive buildings, Sarah Wigglesworth Architects have made a name for themselves as sustainable architects. Sarah and her husband moved into the house in 2000. The garden backs onto a major railway line, not that this is apparent. Enclosed on all sides, it is overshadowed only at one end, and the rest of the space is open and sunny. Emma Griffin was responsible for the design. Her brief was to create a garden that would provide food for the family and allow them to reconnect with the seasons.

1 The greater part of the garden is devoted to vegetable growing. Thought has been given to the varieties planted to ensure continuous cropping. Early raspberry canes 'Glen Moy' are alongside later 'Autumn Bliss', while in the next raised bed potatoes 'Arran Pilot', 'Belle de Fontenay', 'Highland Burgundy Red', 'Salad Blue', and 'Shetland Black' crop in rotation.

2 Sustainability and innovation are key aspects of this project. The house is insulated with straw bales clad in galvanized steel. Water is harvested in water butts. The weathered tree trunk, which appears to be propping up the ceiling, is one of a number of found objects given a new role.

3 The narrow garden has a rural feel, belying its true location. Dividing it up into four raised beds, a seating area, and a decorative shady area highlighted by two birch trees makes it appear much larger. Beds planted with roses and white *Allium nigrum* line the edges and form a visual link to the garden under the birches, where they are joined by *Allium hollandicum* 'Purple Sensation', shown on pages 138–9.

4 Grown as espalier, apples 'Ashmead's Kernel' and 'Laxton's Epicure' and damsons (*Prunus insititia* 'Merryweather Damson') cover the back brick wall. Recycled steel reinforcing rods are used as supports throughout this urban kitchen garden, which even has a hencoop.

FURNISHING THE GARDEN

THE ENRICHMENT OF WATER

From theatrical baroque fountains to the picturesque lakes of the English landscape garden, water features have always been an essential element of garden design. Water can enliven or calm a garden, be smooth and reflective or turbulent and fast-moving. Every garden style, from the formal to the informal, has its own particular vocabulary of water features, from streams to rills, fountains to waterfalls, cascades to weirs, water walls to canals, and ponds to swimming pools and lakes. Natural watercourses, meanwhile, have a romantic charm and are opportunities for individual designs.

1 Nature was the inspiration for this still and reflective pond, fed by a trickle of water, in a garden by Carine Reckinger-Thill.

2 This raised Cor-Ten™ steel water basin by Tom Stuart-Smith is an elegant interpretation of the common water trough.

3 Spencer Viner has created a small water feature, just large enough for a water lily, out of concrete manhole rings stacked on top of each other and finished with a slate rim. The bamboo spout, partly concealed by *Pseudosasa japonica*, lends an Oriental look to the water feature.

4 The question of how to link areas of water to each other has produced some interesting designs. In this garden by Lucy Sommers, a formal water area flows over a stone lip into a pond lined with marginal plants. The transition from the formal to the natural is softened by red-orange *Geum* 'Blazing Sunset' draping over the edge.

5 Seen from above, this jacuzzi, which is also featured on page 35, has the quality of a geyser.

Set off by the light walls and paving, the colour of the water is intensified in this two-tiered town garden designed by Stuart Craine.

6 Emulating nature or enhancing a natural watercourse to make the most of the water supply is one of the great tools of landscape design. At Sandringham House, Norfolk, water is channelled in silvery cascades between rocks and falls into pools flanked by lush water-loving plants, such as gunnera.

1

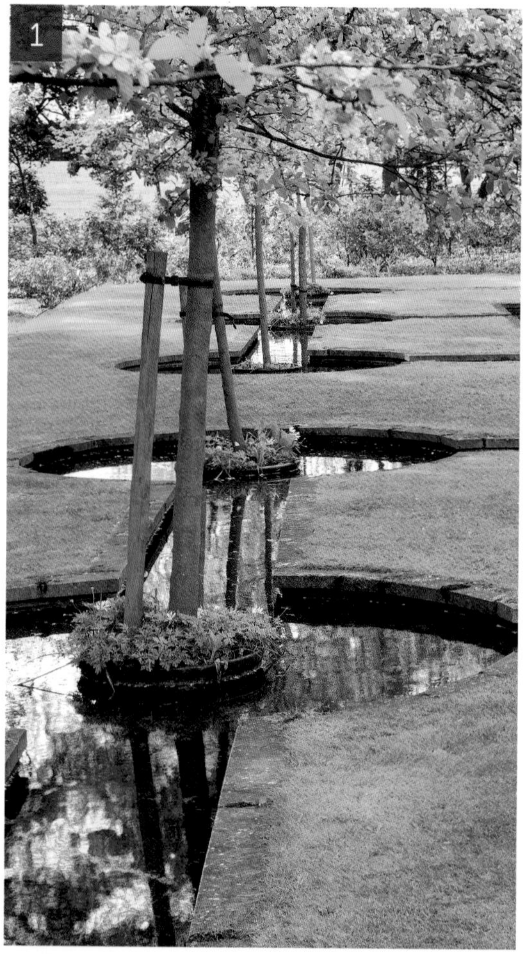

2

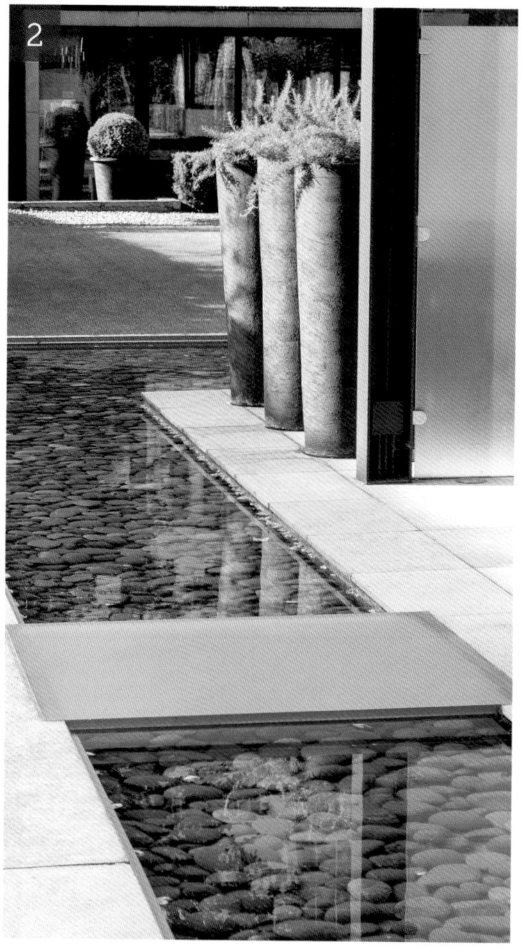

3

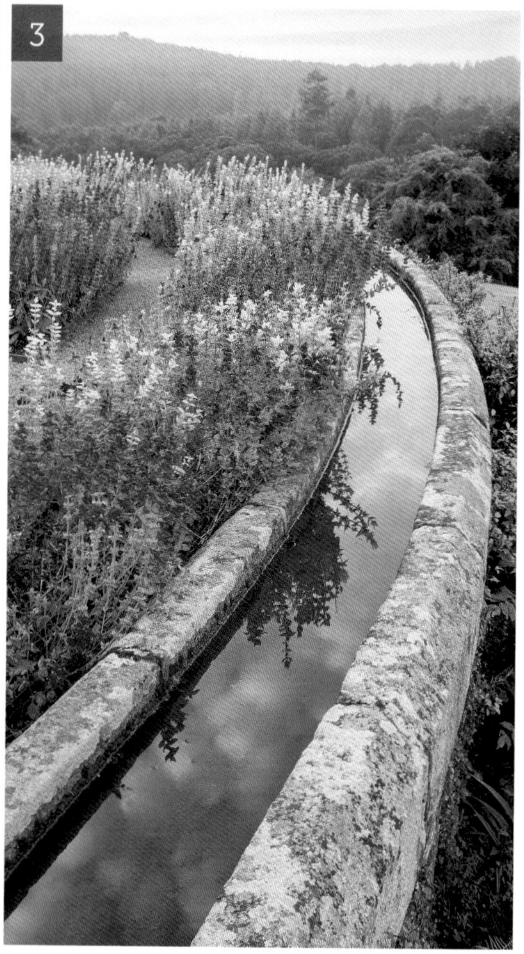

4

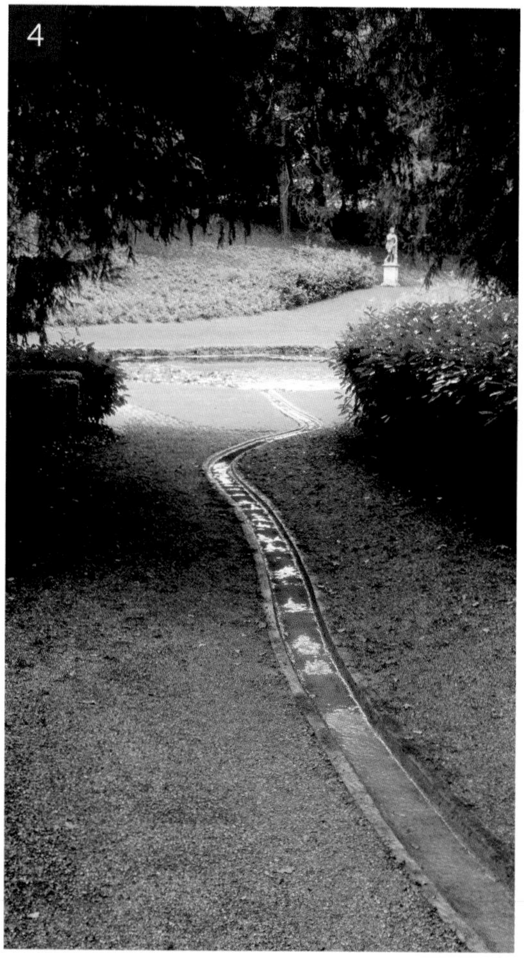

5

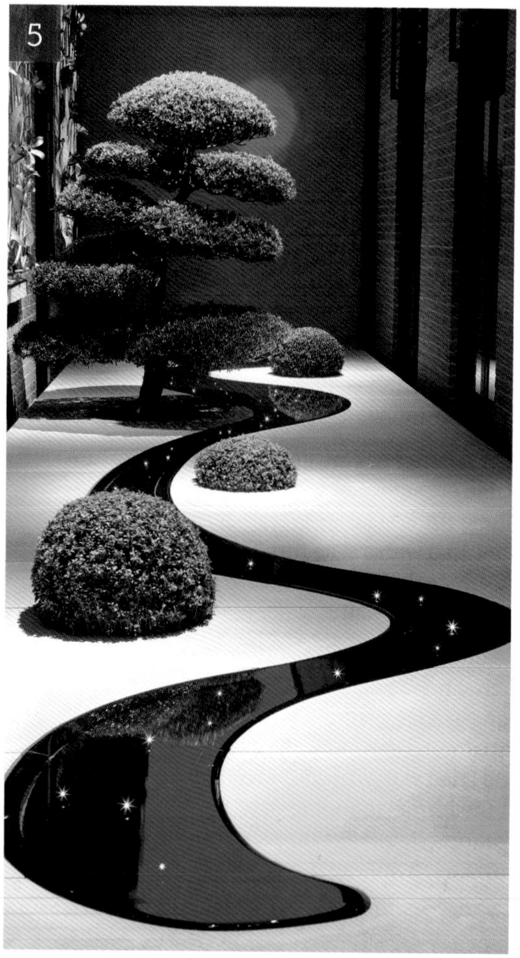

6

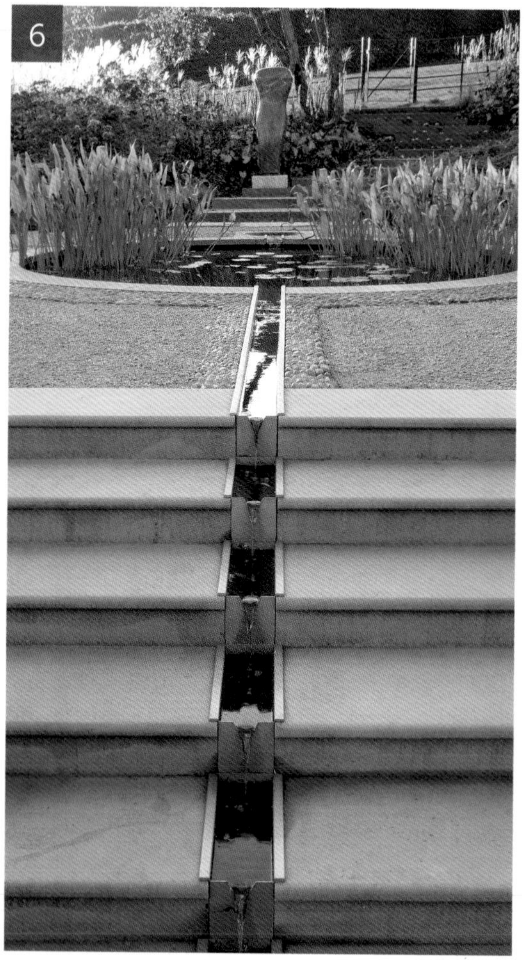

Rills, Canals, and Reflective Pools

Persian and Moorish gardens are marvellous examples of how to use a minimum amount of water for maximum effect. Garden designers have drawn particular inspiration from Granada, Spain – the canals in the Generalife, the reflective pool of the Court of the Myrtles, and the rills in the Court of the Lions at the Alhambra, have all been reinterpreted in contemporary schemes. Water was then, as it is now, a precious commodity to be celebrated and revered.

1 The formal water parterre at West Green House, Hampshire, is a mix of Moorish and baroque styles. Crab apple trees (*Malus* 'Evereste') grow on islands surrounded by circular pools, linked by canals.

2 The flat, reflecting, pebble-lined pools in the Barcelona Pavilion designed by Mies van der Rohe have inspired many contemporary designs. The same tranquil quality has been achieved here by Stuart Craine, who has cleverly laid a glass bridge across the moat-like canal.

3 Rills, narrow channels of water, can divide or enclose. At Endsleigh, Devon, once a hunting lodge and now a hotel, the natural stone rill is wrapped around a flower parterre, separating the garden, which was originally designed in the 19th century by Humphry Repton, from the wider landscape.

4 In the 18th century, William Kent placed rills in an informal manner, rather like drainage channels, down the centre of this path at Rousham House, Gloucestershire.

5 Tom Stuart-Smith has used granite to symbolize water in his design for the Moon Terrace at the Connaught hotel, London.

6 The narrow rill cascading down the steps from the basin breaks the formality of the design and draws the water into this contemporary garden by Anthony Paul.

7 Jacques Wirtz is an expert at creating landscapes that are works of art. In his design for the   du Luxembourg, the simple but elegant circular reflective pool, surrounded by grass, mirrors the seasonal changes.

8 In the same landscape as photograph 7, water snakes its way into the distance. The combination of the crisp edges, carpet of green grass, and vertical trees makes for a strong, graphic effect.

Fountains, Cascades, and Waterfalls

Tumbling and shooting water adds drama to a garden. Depending on the design and setting, fountains and cascades can be spectacular or subtle, a trickle or a torrent. The sound that water makes and the light-bringing and cooling quality it brings as it falls are an essential, but often forgotten, ingredient of garden design.

1 A splay of water is a statement piece that works best as a focal point in a park-like setting. In the 17th-century water garden of Les Jardins d'Annevoie in Belgium, this fountain, framed by hornbeam hedges, takes on an almost modern appearance.

2 Fountains may have fallen out of fashion but that does not mean they have no place in the garden. Piet Oudolf and Arne Maynard's garden for the RHS Chelsea Flower Show in 2000 is still one of the best examples of the use of a single arched jet of water in a contemporary design.

3 Water walls were all the rage a few years ago. Their space-saving attributes and the abstract images caused by water rippling over a polished or mirrored surface, distorting the reflection, made them ideal for small urban gardens. Olivia Kirk's water wall for the 2011 RHS Chelsea Flower Show is set in a wall of dark slate, like an invitation into a mysterious world.

4 A cascade of falling water can mask surrounding sounds. In this Acres Wild design, the water is channelled over a lead lip, to drop as a sheet of water in front of the wall.

5 A stainless-steel waterspout is an elegant and contemporary addition to this garden by Amir Schlezinger.

6 Water gushes from the wall in this Catherine Heatherington waterfall in Liseberg Park, Sweden.

7 Chatsworth in Derbyshire is famous for its grand water staircase. Here, on the garden island of Mainau, Germany, a more domestic version with golden treads looks good even with little water.

8 Flanked by ferns, this waterfall at Hampton Court, Herefordshire, falls into a deep pool, mimicking nature.

Ponds, Pools, and Margins

It is not only shape that determines the look of a sheet of water but also the accompanying planting. Like a veil, reeds, grasses, and other marginal plants soften and blur the edges, giving a more naturalistic look to even a formal pool.

1 Is this a pond, a canal, or a dyke? By alternating stepping stones with hardwood timber 'bridges', Tom Stuart-Smith has altered the proportions and the rhythm of the water area so that it appears to be a series of pools stretching into the distance. Clumps of *Miscanthus sinensis* 'Ferner Osten' soften the sharp edges and bring a marsh-like ambience to the design. Painting or lining a pool black, as here, can create the illusion of depth and provide a dark surface, so that the reflections seem even more brilliant.

2 Balancing planting and water is a challenge. If ponds are too small and shallow, they can quickly be clogged with aquatic plants. Here, the water area is large enough to aerate and for water to flow. The plants have been kept to the edge, creating a mellow, relaxing naturalistic effect in this garden by Acres Wild.

3 A sweeping timber boardwalk leads to a contemplative seating area and seems to restrain the marginal plants on the fringes of the lake at Uggeshall Hall, Suffolk.

4 Swimming pools have moved a long way from the days when they were just turquoise-blue rectangles. The choice available today is immense; from infinity pools, to natural swimming lakes, to pools like the one pictured here – design features in their own right. In Julie Toll's design, every detail is well considered, even the sculptural-like ladder into the pool.

5 The landscape architect Paolo Pejrone is renowned for his bespoke, subtle designs. Here, the rough edge of the pond contrasts with the smooth surface of the water. The heart-shaped leaves of the water lilies are in dialogue with the reflected spears of the foxgloves. This mass of reflected green adds an extra dimension to the garden.

GARDEN FURNITURE AND ACCESSORIES

Benches, chairs, tables, sunshades, and lighting are more than decorative finishing touches – they are the means to enjoy the garden. Furnishing a garden is not so different from furnishing a house, as the right accessories can enhance and underline a style, and also be a focal point. Manufacturers and craftsmen have responded to demand and there now is a wide range of outdoor furniture to suit all styles and sizes of gardens.

1 These timber chairs by Piet Hein Eek are the outdoor equivalent of club chairs – chunky enough to withstand the elements, yet stylish, in keeping with the Piet Oudolf garden.

2 The rattan dining chairs, timber table, and awning make for a chic, relaxed composition in this country garden by Carine Reckinger-Thill. The Baltasar Lobo sculpture, rising out of the planting, has been placed cleverly in the line of vision.

3 Bistro chairs and tables have a particular appeal. This display in Flora Grubb Gardens, San Francisco, illustrates the colour palette of the Fermob range.

4 Crisp and contemporary, the table and the chairs by Barlow Tyrie underline this contemporary coastal design by Jo Thompson.

5 Quirky, metal chairs by Fermob lend an individuality to a Lynne Marcus garden.

6 Jimi Blake opted for a bohemian mix-and-match arrangement of furniture in his garden, and enhanced the bright colours with floral cushions.

Garden Benches

Each part of the garden, from formal seating areas to secluded niches, demands a different type of furniture. Many examples, classic as well as contemporary, are featured throughout this book. While tables and chairs are an ensemble, benches are solitary pieces that can either be tucked away or placed in the spotlight.

1 The classic slatted garden bench has been given a makeover at Sussex Prairies. By merely coordinating the colour with the alliums, the old looks new and fresh.

2 With its contoured seat, Alison Crowther's English oak-rippled bench at the RHS Wisley Gardens, Surrey, is inviting and beautiful – perfect for those quiet moments.

3 Benches, such as this one in George Carter's own garden at Silverstone Farm, Norfolk, can underpin the design concept and also be a focal point.

4 In an imaginative garden for the 2012 RHS Hampton Court Palace Flower Show, Will Sandy has combined a tree guard and yellow lines on either side of the tree to make a metal bench with room for two.

5 This concrete bench by Sydväst arkitektur och landskap in Sweden is a modern, eye-catching take on circular seats commonly found around trees.

6 Supported by stone blocks, this classic timber bench in a Charlotte Rowe garden would be just at home in a formal setting.

7 This contemporary curved oak bench, with a scorched and polished finish, is one of a group of nine memorial seats designed by Jim Partridge and Liz Walmsley for the Bowes-Lyon rose garden at RHS Wisley.

8 The inscription on this bench by Marnie Moyle reads: "What is this life if full of care." It comes from the poem 'Leisure' by W.H. Davies, fitting words for a garden far away from the pressures of city life.

9 The Wave Bench by Anthony Paul sits comfortably in its surroundings, enhanced by the billowing grasses of *Stipa gigantea*.

10 Ben Barrell's crescent-shaped granite bench at Vann, Surrey, adds a contemporary note to this Arts & Crafts garden.

Making Shade

Nothing is more relaxing than sitting in the cool, dappled shade of a tree in summer and looking out over the garden. In the search for the right kind of shade that is neither stifling nor too cool, garden designers and manufacturers have come up with some ingenious solutions, from parasols and sun umbrellas to patio awnings that roll out automatically when the sun becomes too intense.

1 Awnings – tent-like structures spanned between trees or from buildings – are lightweight and cost-effective ways of providing shade over patios, as shown here in a design by Claire Mee.

2 Pergolas have long been favourites for casting shade. They can be freestanding or fixed to the façade, as in this Mondrian-inspired design by Spencer Viner. The shade cast by the rhythmic placing of the beams and metal tubing is an important design element, which brings an extra dimension to the garden.

3 Recognizing the different qualities of shade can enhance a garden or a walkway. In winter and spring, when climbers are dormant, more light will penetrate a pergola. In summer, when climbers such as wisteria, shown in this garden by Lloyd Birchmore and Terry Clare, are in full leaf, the light is blocked and the shade is deeper.

4 Garden parasols come in a variety of shapes, sizes, and colours, from single, cream shades, as in this garden by Anthony Paul Landscape Design, to large, rectangular, Italian market-stall shades. Brightly coloured parasols can be a design statement in their own right.

5 This simple pergola casts a delicate shade and also frames the view into Marion Jay's garden.

6 In central European or southern climates, the shade cast by a tree is hard to beat. In summer, most meals are eaten outdoors, as in this garden by François Valentiny.

7 A delicate metal pergola adds a contemporary note to this lush garden by Catherine Heatherington.

1

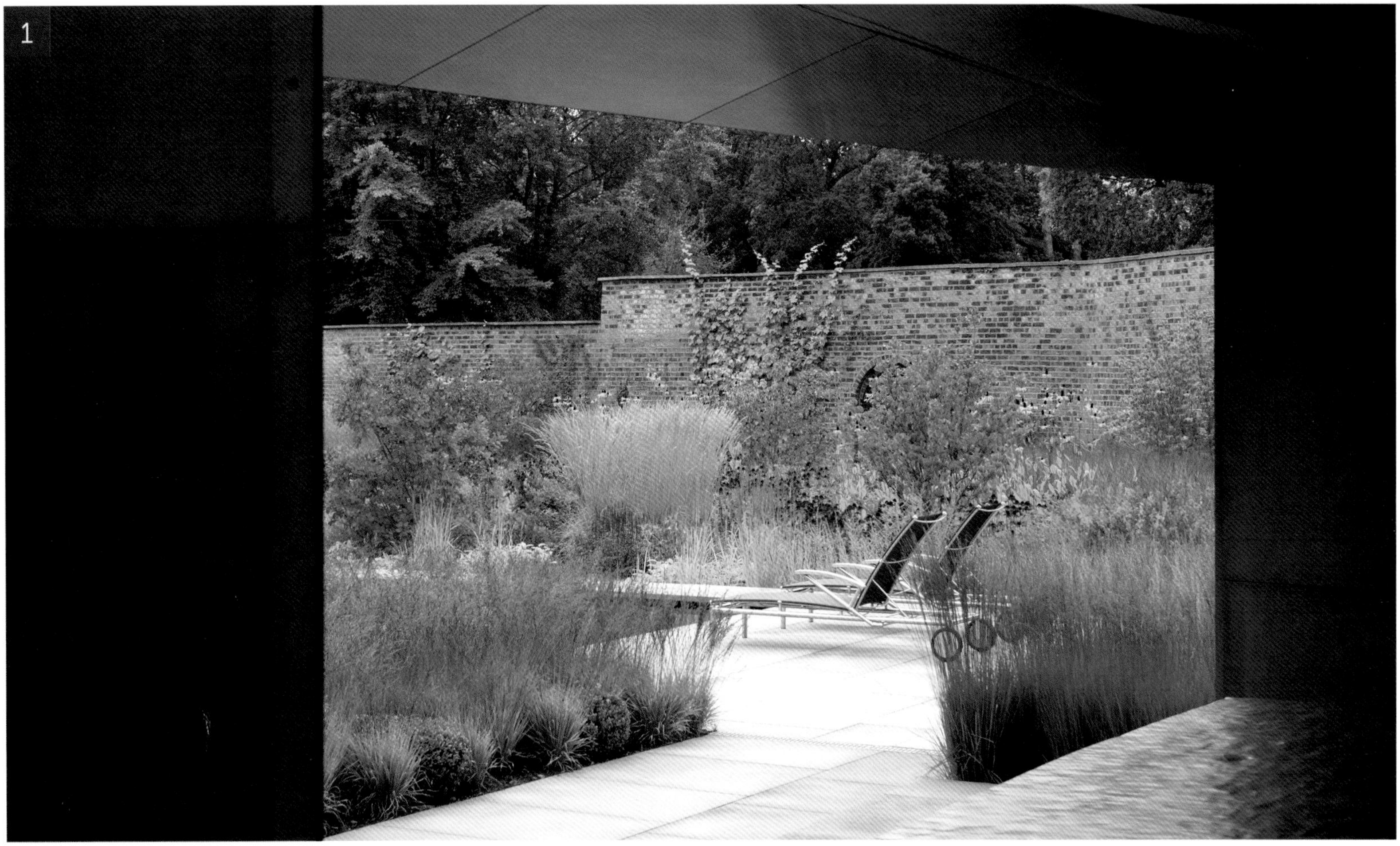

2

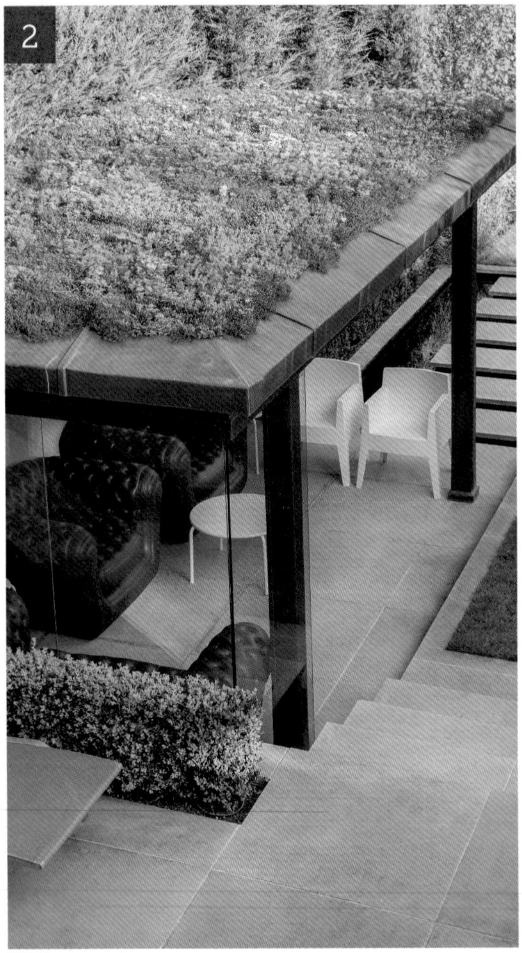

3

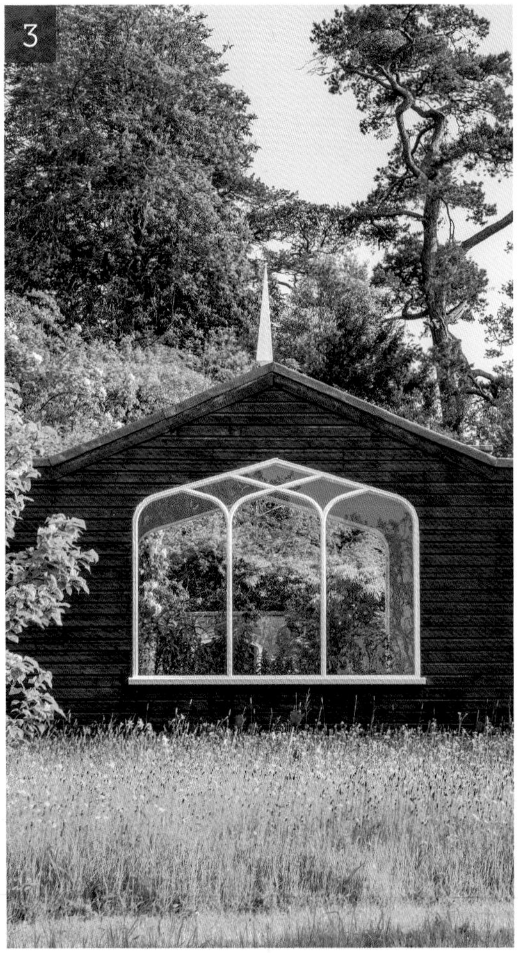

4

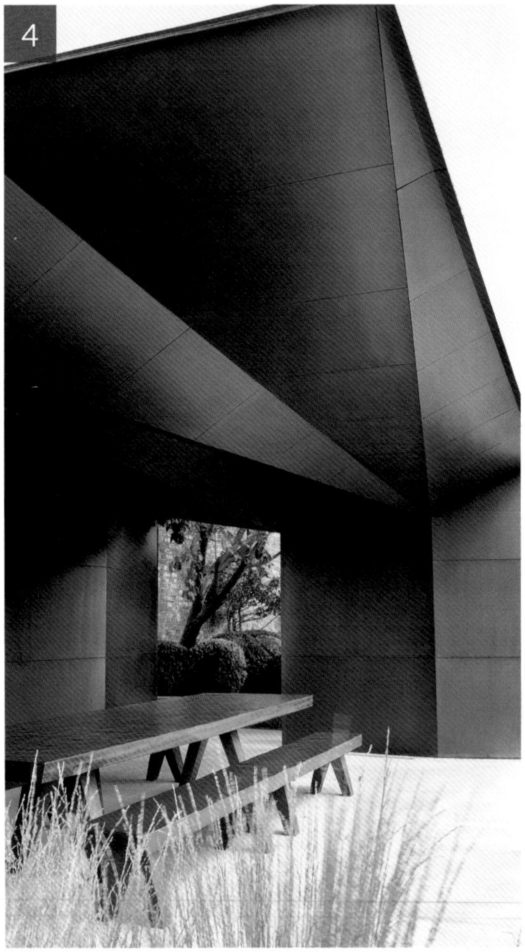

Pavilions, Summerhouses, Sheds, and Follies

Within the hierarchy of ancillary garden buildings, there are those that are necessary, such as sheds and greenhouses, and those that enhance the enjoyment and appreciation of the garden. Gazebos belong in the latter group, as do temple-like pavilions set at the end of a long walk. Each period of garden architecture has its own style of building, from the fanciful to the practical. Although it was once possible to build whatever one wished, planning permission may be required today for larger structures.

1 and 4 In this walled garden in Cheshire, designed by Tom Stuart-Smith, a bold, bronze, origami-like pavilion by the architect Jamie Fobert is both a shelter and a statement piece in the garden. The sculptural qualities of the pavilion are beguiling and contrast with the soft planting. Considering the views from the pavilion into the garden and of the pavilion itself (see photograph 4) is vital if the garden and building are to become one cohesive design.

2 In this design by Lynne Marcus, consideration has been given to the views from all angles. A living green roof of sedums covers the metal-framed pavilion, while the glass panels allow light in and lend a transparency to the structure.

3 The timber-clad summerhouse of the Farnborough Old Rectory, Berkshire, has gothic overtones and a rustic appearance, complementing the setting against the backdrop of trees.

5 Rather than dividing the garden, this glass garden room, part of an L-shaped bungalow designed by Charles Barclay Architects, links the formal lawn area with the wilder garden beyond. The views in the del Buono Gazerwitz garden flow seamlessly, allowing the space to be enjoyed from inside in all weathers.

6 Designed by Lynne Marcus, this simple, contemporary, steel and glass pavilion, with a shimmer of a sedum roof, connects the garden to the landscape beyond.

7 Appearances can be deceptive. By matching the architecture to the planting, this rustic-looking pavilion set among bamboo has the look of a jungle in Borneo, but it is actually at Henstead Exotic Garden, Suffolk. Exotic planting has been discussed on pages 240–3, but accessories are just as important in creating and enhancing the illusion of being in a different world. This timber, pitched-roof pavilion, accessed by timber steps, is a shelter and a lookout over the garden, cleverly designed by Andrew Brogan.

8 At one time, as much thought was given to the design of the gardener's cottage as to the main house. The same goes for pleasure houses and pavilions, which were essential components of European landscape gardens – delightful buildings in which to take tea or, in some cases, bathe. Some, like this pavilion in a Luxembourg kitchen garden, resembled mini-palaces.

9 Potting sheds are wonderful places, taking on a variety of shapes and forms, from the almost palatial at York Gate, near Leeds, where an eye-level circular window looks out onto the garden, to the rustic, timber-clad shed shown here, complete with verandah and garden chairs, at Lowder Mill, Surrey.

10 Garden buildings can be opportunities for unusual designs. Inspired by the architectural details in their house, Zaki and Ruth Elia gave their garden shed Moorish overtones. Complemented by Declan Buckley's lush planting, which includes the large-leaved foxglove tree (*Paulownia tomentosa*) and ferns, the garden could be in a Moroccan riad but is, in fact, in London.

11 This shepherd's hut at Manor Farm, Thixendale, North Yorkshire, has been painted with stripes by Gilda Brader. A nostalgic feature, it imparts a rural air and, because it is on wheels, it can be positioned almost anywhere in the garden and used as a tea hut, playhouse, even storage for tools and animal feed. Like a folly – usually an eccentric building designed to mark a particularly good view or underline an artistic style – the hut has an element of fun about it. Similar movable structures include gypsy caravans, yurts, and exotic tents. In the past, English landscape gardens were fitted with many such temporary structures, all of them for the delight of the owners and their guests.

5

Lighting up the Garden

Garden lighting has come a long way since the 19th century, when driveways of large country houses were lit up by lines of flaming torches. Much later, in the 1980s, it was considered quite daring to have spotlights illuminating trees or even submerged lights in pools. With the advent of LED and energy-efficient lights, a new world of exterior lighting brought gardens and balconies into the 21st century. Longer working hours mean that many city workers only have the opportunity to enjoy their exterior space in the evening. Today's lighting engineers have made this possible, devising a range of solutions for illuminating the outdoors and giving an extra dimension to the garden.

1 Pinpointing which plants to illuminate and how needs careful thought. Much depends on the angle of vision, whether it is from the rooms of the house or the patio. Ideally, the lighting should be an enhancement, regardless of the season and stage of growth. Charlotte Rowe has used uplighters here on a hornbeam (*Carpinus betulus* 'Fastigiata') and *Osmanthus heterophyllus*, playing on the contrasts in shapes and silhouettes.

2 A chain of uplighters casts torch-like shapes on the purple wall, drawing out the contours and colour of the bamboo (*Phyllostachys aureosulcata* f. *aureocaulis*) in this garden designed by Lucy Sommers.

3 In a design by Charlotte Rowe, the shadows cast by the uplighters emphasize the height and texture of the concrete resin pots.

4 Amir Schlezinger is a master of subtle lighting effects. He appreciates that most of the gardens he designs, particularly the inner-city rooftop ones, will be enjoyed primarily at night, and his lighting schemes reflect this. Here, uplighters have been trained on the *Cordyline australis* and the planting in the background.

5 A blue-lit rill, flush with the decking, has the appearance of water in this roof terrace by Claire Mee. Walkover lights are available in a number of forms and are ideal where space is restricted.

1

Garden Highlights

Lighting should be considered in the initial stages of the garden design, as cables have to be laid and power sources determined at the outset. Consult a qualified exterior lighting engineer on the range of lights available, from spotlights and ground spike lights to decking lights and brick lights for incorporating into walls or steps, as well as lighting bollards, wall lights, and LED strips. There are a number of specialist companies that offer valuable advice on outdoor lighting, including Hunza, based in New Zealand, and Bega, in Germany.

The object is not to dazzle or floodlight the garden but to enhance it, contrasting shadows with illuminated areas. Lighting applications vary, with uplighting, crosslighting, downlighting, shadowing, and more to choose from. Much depends on the angle and spread of the light beam. Combining fibre-optic cables into a scheme is also an option but this should be considered at the outset. The beauty of good outdoor lighting is that the light source is unobtrusive but its effect obvious.

1 This Paul Cooper backlit screen in a courtyard has the quality of a work of art. Backlighting, also termed silhouetting, is magical and dramatic, emphasizing outlines and shapes. It can highlight existing trees, as here, or even create illusions of vegetation.

2 Lighting is best when it is subtle and graded, so that tension is created between dark and light areas, to add a sense of mystery and depth to the garden. Areas of water and changes in levels should be highlighted for safety reasons if the garden is to be used at night. Pinpricks of light can be effective and attractive. Light pollution is often irritating, so consideration for neighbours and regulating the light display are paramount. In this garden by Adam Shepherd, also featured on pages 306–7, the underside of the trees and taller perennials are highlighted, while the rest of the garden disappears into the night.

3 Twilight is the magical end to the day. Uplighters trained on these palms (*Trachycarpus fortunei*) at Henstead Exotic Garden, Suffolk, have extended the time that the garden can be enjoyed, and this additional layer of lighting creates a romantic atmosphere.

Art in the Garden

When works of art – whether paintings, reliefs, sculptures, or conceptual art – are displayed in galleries, they are in a neutral environment, where they are allowed to shine. But in gardens, they are vying for attention with so many other things that the art can so easily come across as tat.

Evaluating and deciding what role art should play in the garden is key to its successful staging. The garden's design should enhance the artwork and vice versa. In classical gardens, figures were often set apart on plinths in tranquil positions, displayed in niches or against a neutral backdrop of hedging, where they could look their best and be admired without distraction. Sculpture should not perch but sit happily in the surroundings. Art in the garden need not be grand but it does have to be fitting, and regardless of its size, it needs space to breathe.

1 Staging and scale are vital when incorporating art into gardens. Glistening "Flying Saucers" by Robin Johnson, shown here at Sussex Prairies, do not jar with their surroundings but interact with it, weaving in and out of the matt, bronze grasses of *Panicum virgatum* 'Shenandoah'.

2 By positioning the "Flock of Seagulls" by Jack Trowbridge between bushes of *Spiraea* 'Arguta' and staggering the heights, Marion Stanley has evoked the image of birds flying over clouds in her garden at Mazey Cottage, Cornwall.

3 The placement of art is paramount. In this Christopher Bradley-Hole garden, a delicate carpet of blonde-bronze grasses sets off the strong organic, cocoon-like shape of the sculptural seat by Ron Arad. The rough contrasts with the smooth, and the man-made with the natural. There is a generosity of space here and a sense of discovery, which enhance both the art and the garden.

4 A herd of Cor-Ten™ weathered steel buffalo sculptures marches off into the distance at Sussex Prairies. The templates were designed by Pauline McBride and laser-cut by a specialist firm. The motif is particularly apt for this garden, which takes its cue from the North American prairies.

11

5 Some art is predestined for pole position in the garden. This "Hollopod" oak sculpture by Si Uwins has a subtle beauty to it and has been masterfully embedded in a planting of *Rudbeckia fulgida* var. *sullivantii* 'Goldsturm' at Sussex Prairies. The button-like seed heads echo the larger round openings in the sculpture, which appear even more dramatic against a backdrop of *Molinia caerulea* subsp. *arundinacea* 'Karl Foerster'.

6 Art works best when there is a dialogue between it and the surroundings. In a border designed by Aileen Scoular, the variegation of the heart-shaped leaves of *Brunnera macrophylla* 'Jack Frost' appears even lighter against Jim Whitson's matt lead, seed pod sculpture.

7 Denmans in West Sussex is the garden of John Brookes, the garden designer and author of the pivotal garden design book *Room Outside*. A testimony to his philosophy, Denmans is a showcase of how art can be incorporated into the garden without it being imposing or dominating. The light green leaves of an Indian bean tree (*Catalpa bignonioides* 'Aurea') and a mound of dark green glossy leaved × *Fatshedera lizei* flank the bird sculptures by Marion Smith, which appear simply to be resting in the garden.

8 Using recycled products to create garden features is nothing new. However, they are rarely successful because they are so often conceived in isolation and without the surroundings in mind. Claire Woodbine's artistic talent shines through at Pinsla Garden, Cornwall, where a number of her artworks, including this plant-pot snake, are secreted in the woodland.

9 Both in silhouette and at close range, this bronze sculpture by Michael Speller, aptly named "Presence", is dramatic. It is a centrepiece that works best against a light wall and with minimal planting. In keeping her patio design uncluttered and pared-back, Lynne Marcus has created both tension and harmony.

10 Oversized walnut sculptures of reconstituted stone by the Landscape Ornament Company are scattered in the shade of a walnut tree in Jeannine Sponville's Luxembourg garden. In general for these kinds of display, groups of three placed in a loose triangle are more pleasing than rigid arrangements.

11 The abstract quality of this rusted metal upright sculpture by Josiane Marschal contrasts with the birch, adding another dimension to the garden designed by Marie-Jeanne Schumacher-Putz.

12 Landscape and art come together in this park-like garden. The strong, vertical white trunks of the stand of birches contrast with the delicate metal rings of Bruno Romeda's sculpture. The parallel rills set in the grass reflect the circles and mirror the sky, acting almost as an uplighter, highlighting the underside of the metal. When standing in front or behind the rings, a different effect is achieved. Then, as if looking through spectacles, the view is framed and attention is focused on the distance. Large-scale, three-dimensional art and installations should be admired from all angles, presenting not just one picture but several. Gardens like this, designed by Carine Reckinger-Thill, rely on creating an ambience where art and landscape complement each other.

13 A bright red wall with niches for sculpted heads terminates the vista of this London garden designed by Gordon McArthur and Paul Thompson. The equally spaced sculptures, sourced from Stoned and Plastered at Columbia Road Flower Market, London, are much more powerful viewed as a group than individually. Enveloped by vegetation, the colour of the wall seems bolder and the shadows darker, highlighting the recesses and propelling the sculptures to the foreground.

14 Small-scaled works of art can so easily look kitschy in the garden, but what prevents this is choosing the right setting and exercising restraint, to avoid an overload of images and objects. Here, fish sculptures by Nancy Train Smith float effortlessly over a sea of *Pachysandra terminalis* in a Massachusetts garden designed by Nan Sinton.

15 A Cor-Ten™ weathered steel sculpture by Roger Platts rises out of the planting like giant wood shavings. The thin, linear steel is echoed in the blades of the adjoining phormium, which seems to wrap itself around the base of the sculpture.

16 The Hungarian French sculptor Marta Pan (1923–2008) was renowned for her simple yet bold, large, organic-shaped outdoor sculptures. Mostly white or red, they were made out of glass fibre reinforced with polyester resin and were often conceived for a particular location. Here, the dialogue with the surroundings is all-important: the contrast between the organic form and the geometric hedges, and the opening and closing of space all create a dynamic interchange between the garden and the art, which is vital if the pieces are to have any meaning in their setting. "Floating Sculpture 3" by Pan, with a similar aperture, is exhibited on a lake at The Hakone Open-Air Museum, Japan.

15

16

DIFFICULT PLOTS AND TRICKS OF THE TRADE

ON THE ROOF

As major cities expand upwards, increasing numbers of high-density apartment blocks, many with roof gardens, are being constructed. These outdoor spaces are being transformed by talented designers into imaginative and exciting gardens that cater for their clients' lifestyles.

While the design and construction of private roof gardens is a comparatively new profession, the commercial sector has been greening roofs for a number of years. Building a roof garden is like adding another storey: the flat roof must be capable of supporting the load and constructed accordingly. Heavy items such as trees must be placed over load-bearing areas, and a structural engineer should always be consulted.

1 A transparent barrier allows light and air into this narrow section of a balcony-cum-roof garden that is split into several different spaces, interlinking the inside with the outside. In this section, Amir Schlezinger has opted for a simple band of *Lavandula angustifolia* 'Melissa Lilac' in an elegant, long and narrow bespoke planter.

2 The protruding roof light has been cleverly made into a feature in this design by Sam Martin. Making a cohesive interesting design on flat roofs, where there are so many constraints, is a challenge. Here, curved raised beds hug the edge, and Astroturf has been laid as a carpet abutting the decking – a lightweight and good-looking solution.

3 The glass doors create a seamless transition between the exterior and interior of the penthouse in this Fiona Naylor design. It is simple but effective, with decking, gravel, a contorted willow (*Salix babylonica* 'Tortuosa'), bamboo, and lavender.

4 In response to the arid conditions common to most roof gardens, Lynne Marcus has opted for a drought-tolerant planting of *Verbena bonariensis*, *Anemanthele lessoniana*, and a roof-garden favourite, lavender.

5 Amir Schlezinger has deservedly earned a reputation for his stylish roof gardens. Here, he has created a simple, elegant example for use during the day, and also in the evening, as shown on page 278.

Extensive or Intensive Planting?

A variety of solutions have been developed for greening roofs. The flat roofs of large commercial units that are visible from above generally have an extensive carpet of sedum, rockery-type plants, or meadows. These plants respond well to the extreme conditions – drought and prolonged exposure to the sun and wind – found on roofs. Smaller roof gardens with direct access to living quarters tend to be intensively greened, with a mixture of hard surfaces and raised beds.

Simply covering a roof with soil and then planting is not an option. There are many aspects to consider. Guidelines exist that take into account the construction of the roof and the depth of substrate and other layers required for the various types of planting to ensure that any roof landscaping is structurally sound and will not cause any building damage. Weight, drainage, and access are the main issues. It is not unusual for cranes to be used to hoist large specimen plants up onto a roof. The size and weight limits of an elevator are also a determining factor.

1 Balancing planting with the hard landscape is key to successful roof gardens. Secondary features such as railings and balustrades also play an important role. In this multi-level roof garden in London, designed by Amir Schlezinger, the horizontal stainless-steel rails contrast with the strongly defined shapes of the arid-loving planting of *Libertia ixioides* 'Goldfinger' and *Hebe* 'Clear Skies'.

2 In this Emma Griffin and Sarah Wigglesworth Architects design, also shown on pages 256–7, the meadow of oxeye daisies is a vast improvement on the average inner-city rooftop.

3 As there is little planting depth to play with on roof gardens, raised beds and planters have an important role. Designers such as Christopher Bradley-Hole are well versed at achieving the maximum effect within restricted planting depths. On this roof terrace, ornamental grasses make a dramatic statement, acting as a windbreak as well as a decorative feature.

4 Collections of terracotta pots in different sizes, as on this Venetian roof terrace, are commonplace in many southern European cities and towns, where flat roofs are part of the design language of buildings.

USING POTS AND PLANTERS

Roof gardens, balconies, entrances to buildings, window boxes, and small courtyards are all potted plant territory. Pots are often a way of growing plants that are unsuited to either the climate or the soil. As to what type of container to use, that depends on the overall design, the location, as well as the climate.

Large Cretan terracotta pots are magnificent but cannot withstand heavy, prolonged frosts. The same applies to most glazed pots. Barrels are popular for rustic appeal, while timber, Versailles-type planters look the part in classic gardens. In addition to traditional plant pots, there is now a range of modern forms, some made to order, with in-built irrigation systems and water reservoirs, which all open up the possibilities for the potted garden.

1 Virtually anything can be used as a plant container, the only provisos being that the plants do not become waterlogged or are heated up and "cooked" by poor insulation. Vegetables growing in an assortment of containers are shown on page 255. In this design by Edwina Roberts, pink-blonde-leaved *Heuchera* 'Crème Brûlée' is growing in a metal dustbin.

2 In inner cities, where a network of cables, pipes, and drains under pavements prevents anything from being planted into the ground, containers and raised beds are the only way to green the streets. Arterra Landscape Architects have transformed the wide pavement on this typically steep San Francisco street into a garden. Cor-Ten™ weathered steel raised beds have been staggered up the slope and planted with

Anemanthele lessoniana and red-flowering kangaroo paw (*Anigozanthos*).

3 Lead planters used in historic gardens were supplanted first by cast iron, then by galvanized steel containers, which can be made in a variety of forms and finishes. Amir Schlezinger is making a name for himself with his inventive, bespoke planters that are pieces of sculpture in their own right. How they are planted is just as important as their looks, and thought is given to the smallest details. *Euphorbia characias* subsp. *wulfenii* alternates with *Stipa gigantea* in this planter, which is topped with gravel.

4 Copper plant pots with chives and violas lend an Oriental note to this vegetable garden by Helen and James Dooley.

Mobile Greenery and Statement Pots

Moving pots around, changing the content with the seasons, or bringing tender plants out of winter quarters are all part of the fun of gardening. Pots can freshen and enliven a garden, be a feature, a backdrop, or even a screen. They can take on a formal air or evoke memories of the countryside. Nantes, in France, transformed and enhanced a number of its inner-city streets with building bags filled with inventive, avant-garde plant displays. Such instant, playful containers are an inspiration and could have a place in urban gardens.

1 Helen Dillon has been making a case for gardening with containers for a number of years. For her Dublin garden, she has chosen galvanized steel dustbins, available from any good hardware store, and black plastic pots – she finds these less intrusive than designer pots and more suited to being shifted around the garden for bulking up a bed or for gathering in groups alongside the house. *Cosmos bipinnatus*, *Senecio cristobalensis*, *Melianthus major*, and *Ensete ventricosum*, with its exotic foliage, flank the central rill that runs through the garden, and add depth and interest to the planting beds. Plants in containers can be overwintered in the greenhouse, allowing Helen to indulge her passion for exotic and unusual foliage that would not normally survive the Irish winters.

2 A more classical look has been achieved in this London garden by del Buono Gazerwitz Landscape Architecture. The tricky area in front of the basement window has been transformed by planting rhythmic rows of clipped box balls in terracotta pots.

3 Statement planters are almost works of art. Custom-made for this niche on a roof garden designed by Amir Schlezinger, also shown on page 292, the hollow, square container, planted with spiky *Dasylirion serratifolium*, is bold enough to compete with the city panorama.

4 Claire Mee has an eye for unusual pots and containers that complement her contemporary garden designs. Conic vases from Ateliér Vierkant in Belgium are filled with white-flowering *Narcissus* 'Thalia' and soft, overhanging muehlenbeckias.

EXTREME GARDENING

Gardening at high altitudes, on the coast, or in arid regions calls for determination and vision. Making a garden in extreme conditions is a challenge but, when successful, produces gardens of great beauty and invidiality.

Looking at the natural habitat of these areas, where plants have to be tough and resilient to withstand the conditions, can be a source of inspiration. In coastal gardens, protection from the wind is essential, and shelter belts are often planted before the garden is laid out. These may comprise several layers to create an inner core that the ripping, salt-laden winds cannot penetrate.

1 An arid region is one of the most challenging environments in which to create a garden yet, even in these dry conditions, exciting sustainable gardens are possible. In this Shades of Green design in California, *Ceanothus* 'Dark Star', has been combined with rows of *Lavandula* × *intermedia* 'Grosso'.

2 Few visitors to St Michael's Mount in Cornwall venture into the stunning garden that is staggered over terraces on the opposite side of the main path leading up the mount. Gardeners here must be able to rock-climb and abseil, as well as being familiar with tender plants that would not normally survive in Britain. The island has its own microclimate; it is far warmer and sunnier than the mainland, which allows plants such as aeoniums, *Echeveria elegans*, *E. affinis*, and razor-sharp *Agave americana* to flourish on the scree slope of the upper levels.

3 Planting along seaside promenades has developed little since Edwardian times but Bexhill-on-Sea in East Sussex is an exception. "Next Wave", a 600-m (656-yard) long mixed herbaceous border designed by Noel Kingsbury, shows what is possible in salty, windy, arid conditions. Taking his cue from nature, Noel selected tough, wiry plants that are attractive in all seasons. In the section shown here, divided and protected by a timber wall, *Eryngium bourgatii*, *Helichrysum italicum*, tufts of *Carex comans* bronze-leaved, *Santolina chamaecyparissus*, and *Salvia nemorosa* 'Ostfriesland' form an undulating, close-knit ground cover.

4 Seaside gardening is an art. It is also more than a question of what will survive in the conditions but also of what will best blend into and reflect the wider landscape. By using tall plants and grasses, such as *Verbena bonariensis* and *Anemanthele lessoniana*, Declan Buckley has brought the maritime look right up to the house, creating an enclosed seating area that works well with the contemporary building by Richard Paxton Architects.

Gardening on the Edge

Endurance, tenacity, patience, and a respect for the elements are all prerequisites for coastal gardening. Any thoughts of a conventional garden have to be abandoned in favour of a tamed wild look that draws in the wider landscape.

1 Set on the edge of a nature reserve near Rye, East Sussex, this weekend retreat is a magical place but it was not necessarily the best place to make a garden in the first place. Exposed, on shifting shingle, and pummelled by salt-laden winds, little survived here. A Channel 4 television series came to the rescue of the then owners, Wendy Booth and Leslie Howell. Dan Pearson planted a shelter belt of *Elaeagnus × ebbingei*. Abandoned timber groynes from a nearby beach were brought into the garden and used for raised beds and terracing. Drought-tolerant plants such as sea holly and santolina were introduced and slowly the garden took shape. Like all of this exceptional garden (also shown in photographs 2 and 5), the pond, dotted with yucca, phormiums, *Stipa tenuissima*, and *S. gigantea*, is very much part of the surrounding landscape.

2 and 5 A romantic, dreamy atmosphere pervades the 0.3-hectare (¾-acre) garden. Many plants, like the *Centranthus ruber*, Californian poppies (*Eschscholzia californica*), and *Papaver rhoeas*, self-seed among the driftwood sculptures by the house. Attention to detail here is important; even the paving is in keeping with the coastal feel of the place.

3 and 4 Chygurno garden in Cornwall should not really exist. Clinging onto a steep slope, the only bit of flat land is next to the house. This is hard-core, extreme gardening, as everything has to be manhandled up and down the slope. Despite this, the owners have created an amazing garden full of rare and unusual plants in wonderful combinations. It is unusual for a property to be chosen on the basis of its soil, but Chygurno was. A passion for rhododendrons and other acid-loving plants led the owners to create a garden that is quite exceptional.

6 Christopher Holliday's garden overlooking Morecambe Bay, Lancashire, takes advantage of the microclimate and even combats the salty winds to make a garden full of beauty, with plants such as phormiums and *Cortaderia richardii*.

AWKWARD SPACES

In inner cities, where space is at a premium, even the dingiest, smallest, most awkwardly shaped outdoor area is worth saving and transforming, but it takes ingenuity to come up with meaningful designs for them. As many of the best ideas are in private gardens, hidden from view, it is often difficult to experience them. However, contemporary hotels and upmarket offices are good sources of inspiration for these neglected spaces, as are the pages of international lifestyle magazines such as *AD* and *Elle Decor*.

1 Patrick Blanc's vertical green gardens enhance the urban landscapes of many French innercity environments and now an example can be found in London. The facade of the Driver, a restaurant in Kings Cross, has been transformed into a vibrant living green wall covered in a multitude of species including pink *Centranthus ruber*.

2 It is almost impossible to come up with effective designs for extremely narrow, tall, and enclosed spaces. Increasingly, these areas are overlooked, often by offices or, as here, by a bedroom, so they do deserve more attention. Light reflected from windows adds more light to a space, as do polished surfaces and pale-coloured walls. Marie Clarke's design picks up on all these aspects and more: the vertical element of the space – yellow-stemmed bamboo in containers underplanted with lush *Soleirolia soleirolii* – transforms the void into a tranquil garden.

3 This narrow, shaded garden has been transformed into a green oasis by Christopher Masson. Layering the plants, and contrasting different shapes and textures, has achieved such a sense of depth that it is impossible to tell where the garden ends.

4 Shoehorned between buildings and garden walls, the exterior space of this terraced townhouse in London is hardly more than a light well. Fiona Heyes has managed to salvage the situation and created an elegant outdoor room. By seamlessly linking the interior and exterior spaces, both appear fairly generous and less cramped. Perhaps more by chance than design, the horizontal pattern of the CD-rack is echoed in the slats of the timber cladding, serving to pull the two areas together. Defining the seating area with natural stone, which almost acts as a rug, adds light and interest to the scheme, as does the mirror on the right-hand garden wall. Planting is minimal and considered, with white *Tulipa* 'White Triumphator' in the raised bed acting like pinpricks of light.

1

Courtyards, Basements, and Leftover Spaces

Basements, voids, and light shafts are some of the most difficult spaces to design. They are normally in the rain shadow and therefore dry, most certainly shaded, and frequently unattractive. Optimizing space, recognizing potential, and altering proportions, so that the area appears larger, brighter, and more interesting, are all tools that garden designers use to produce the best possible schemes.

Often these are the simplest. Plants are an option, not a must. Using hard landscape, water, and a vertical sculpture, whether freestanding or a wall relief, can be just as effective as a jungle-type solution using masses of plants.

1 Shelves have been staggered up the stairwell of this inner-city dwelling, providing space for an assortment of potted plants, with wires spanned above them for climbers. The design is neither overloaded nor cluttered but considered.

2 Digging down to gain additional living space has almost become the norm in cities. In this garden designed by Modular, the planting in the void has been kept simple, with a bushy, feathery-leaved *Podocarpus salignus* at one end and a climbing hydrangea poking over the top of the wall. Glass screens enclose the area but also allow light in. Reflected light from the windows increases the brightness of the space, which allows a greater range of plants to grow – a phenomenon that is also common in inner-city courtyards that are enclosed by high buildings.

3 The front garden of this London house was reconfigured in an effort to increase the light fall into the lower-ground floor and simultaneously block out views from the street. Henrietta Courtauld's elegant and refined design has also enhanced the view from the basement room. A tall yew hedge, along with two magnolias, screens the garden at street level. The void to the lower-ground floor has been pushed further into the garden, retained and tanked by a stone wall. Rows of clipped box line the bottom of the void, enhancing the space and incorporating it into the overall design.

CASE STUDY

The Long and Narrow

Only 4.6m (15ft) wide but 20m (65½ft) long, the proportions of this plot are typical of many terraced-house gardens in London. Adam Shepherd was asked to transform and reconfigure the space. Access to the garage at the rear was vital, as was a link to the reception rooms on the raised ground floor. The final beguiling design, which employs devices that add layers of interest to the garden, is both simple and complex.

1 Pages 288–9 show the intimate side of the garden, with framed views and arching canopies. In this view from the balcony, the garden seems to be pushed into the distance, while its width is accentuated. Brazilian, black riven slate paving is spliced by darker, flush drainage channels, like train tracks, forming a strong graphic motif. A subtle change in levels is signalled by a dark horizontal line that also delineates different areas: the borders at the back, the open patio in the middle, and the ipe hardwood planters, which double up as seating, at the front in the sunny part of the garden. Adam likes to bring plants closer to the house. As he says, "Like a giant outdoor vase, they are the first layer of a theatrical 'set'." Filtering views through screens such as the birch tree adds an air of mystery and depth to the garden.

2 Purple-reds and greens are dominant colours in the finely composed planting, where foliage is as important as flowers.

3 *Acer palmatum* 'Bloodgood', underplanted with, among others, *Persicaria amplexicaulis* 'Rosea' in the foreground, frames and filters the view back to the house.

4 Creating spaces for different functions is the mark of this remarkable garden. A seating area is demarcated by the dark line of the drainage channel and furnished with contemporary chairs.

5 The way in which access from the upper-ground floor to the garden has been incorporated into the design is ingenious. A balcony leads along the high boundary fence of Western red cedar, past the beautifully textured vertical planting, to a stainless-steel staircase. Colour has been handled well and with imagination throughout the garden, with warm russets contrasting with the matt anthracite paving and lush green vegetation, to create an enveloping warm glow.

CREATING ILLUSIONS

A garden is an illusion, a refuge, a private place where we can create our ideal world, separate from everyday life. Over the centuries, architects and designers have employed various tactics to manipulate the perception of space and deceive the viewer. One such example, popular in the 18th century, is the ha-ha. This hidden retaining wall with a ditch was an essential device in landscape gardens, which allowed barrier-free views over parkland but prevented livestock from wandering near the house. Landscape designer Humphry Repton suggested that smaller breeds of cattle and sheep grazing in the fields would trick the eye into thinking the landscape was far larger than it was.

1 By breaking up the change in level into three sections, Declan Buckley has not only managed to "stretch" this garden but has also created the illusion that it continues off to the side. The vista to the zinc pot is framed by lush planting, including *Neopanax laetus* and *Euphorbia mellifera*, giving an exotic air. Gurgling water from the pump in the pot masks the sound of the city, heightening the sense of being in a place apart.

2 and 3 A hornbeam hedge encloses the seating area, and shelters views into the narrow garden. While the seating area is paved formally in a herringbone pattern, the meandering path is randomly laid in flint, intersected with brick strips. S-shaped paths were used in landscape gardens in order to extend the promenade and thus make the

garden appear larger. Del Buono Gazerwitz Landscape Architecture have adopted the principle in this contemporary urban garden, which is enhanced by the "Loop" concrete outdoor lounger, designed in 1954 by Willy Guhl.

4 George Carter has drawn on classical rules of staging a view in Marianne Majerus's small garden. Tall blocks of holly hedges, like stage wings, are staggered on either side of the central axis, thereby altering the garden's proportions. It appears to be wider and, like a theatre, there is a sense of mystery as to what is hidden in the wings. Rows of box balls in pots strengthen the vista, as do the horizontal lines of the brick steps. The fountain, set in a shell grotto, is in the shade, which also adds to the illusion of depth.

Borrowing and Framing Views

The advent of perspective in Renaissance painting had a major impact on all forms of art, including garden architecture. The formal gardens of the Renaissance, with their framed views and vistas within the garden and to the countryside beyond, became the benchmark for garden designers. Gardens are the ultimate expression of three-dimensional art: spaces created to please, lead the eye, and evoke a sense a place. Historical gardens are a great source of inspiration, as each epoch has developed its own distinct style of enhancing and incorporating views.

Taking advantage of surrounding or neighbouring scenery – "borrowing" the landscape – is a design tool that has been used for centuries. In traditional Japanese gardens, it is a vital component known as *shakkei*. Framed views in English landscape gardens are used as a reward, a means to tempt the visitor to venture further. Other devices can be used to create illusions of size or grandeur, such as trompe l'oeil murals. Designed to deceive the eye, they depict garden scenes and plants, often with exaggerated perspective, and were popular at the beginning of the 20th century, particularly in France. A number of elegant trompe l'oeils can be found in private gardens on the Côte d'Azur, such as the beautiful tiled examples at Les Colombières, designed by Ferdinand Bac.

1 Borrowing and framing come together in this clairvoyée at Wickham Place Farm, Essex. Apertures, either oval or round as here, with or without ornamental ironwork, are windows onto the surroundings. This view is of an ancient wisteria, one of the largest in the country, while in the opposite direction it is of woodland.

2 Who would think that this is a swimming pool? It is not only its shape but also its position on a terrace at Kiftsgate Court, overlooking the Vale of Evesham, with the Malvern Hills in the distance, that make it appear so much more. Diany Binny laid out the pool in the 1960s, but the decision by her daughter to paint the lining black was the finishing touch to the ensemble.

3 Gardening in difficult conditions, such as on poor soils or on exposed sites, is frustrating but worthwhile if the effort is rewarded by a magnificent view of the landscape, as in Jessica Duncan's Devon garden. Creating a personal picture is, in the end, what making a garden is all about.

1

INDEX

ACKNOWLEDGEMENTS

Design Credits

Page numbers are displayed in **bold**, image numbers in *italic*. 'D' indicates the designer of a garden or an artwork/sculpture.

Front cover D: Tom Stuart-Smith, GB **Back cover** D: Emma Griffin Garden Design, GB. Pitman Tozer Architects, GB **Endpapers** D: Christopher Bradley-Hole, GB **2–3** June Blake's Garden, IE. D: June Blake, IE **4–5** Sleightholmedale Lodge, GB. D: Rosanna James, GB **6** D: Declan Buckley Design Associates, GB **8–9** D: Emma Griffin Garden Design, GB **10–11** *1* D: Chris Ghyselen, BE; *2* The High Line, NY, US. D: James Corner (Field Operations), Diller Scofidio + Renfro, Piet Oudolf, NL; *3* D: Anthea Fortescue, GB; *4* Sea Gem, Camber Sands, GB. D: Jo Thompson, GB **12–13** *1* Eccleston Square Gardens, GB; *2* D: Flora Grubb Gardens, US; *3* Trevoole Farm, GB. D: Beth Stevens, GB; *4* D: Chris Ghyselen, BE **14–15** *1* D: Piet Oudolf, NL; *2* Gravetye Manor, GB; *3* D: David Hicks, GB; *4* Sleightholmedale Lodge, GB **16–17** *2* D: Rachel James, GB; *3* Fairhaven Woodland Garden Trust, GB; *5* Chygurno, GB **18–19** *1* D: Spencer Viner, North Eleven Garden Design, GB; *2* Manor House Farm, Norfolk, GB; *3* D: Richard Holden Architects, GB, Sam Martin Exterior Architecture, GB; *4* D: Arterra Landscape Architects, US; *5* D: Declan Buckley Design Associates, GB, Dan Cooper, GB **20–21** *1* D: Amir Schlezinger, MyLandscapes, GB **22–23** *1, 2, 3, 5* D: Marc Schoellen, LU; *4, 6* Gravetye Manor, GB **24–25** D: Tom Stuart-Smith, GB **26–27** *1* D: Sara Jane Rothwell, London Garden Designer, GB; *2* D: Sam Martin Exterior Architecture, GB; *3* The Manor House, Ayot St Lawrence, GB. D: Julie Toll Landscape & Garden Design, GB; *4* D: François Valentiny, HVP Architects, LU **28–29** *1, 2, 3* June Blake's Garden, IE. D: June Blake, IE **30–31** *1, 2, 3* D: del Buono Gazerwitz Landscape Architecture, GB **32–33** *1, 2, 3* D: Spencer Viner, North Eleven Garden Design, GB **34–35** *1* D: Declan Buckley Design Associates, GB; *2, 4* D: Charlotte Rowe Garden Design, GB; *3* D: Stuart Craine Design, GB, Dyer Grimes Architects, GB **36–37** *1, 2, 3* D: Charlotte Rowe Garden Design, GB **38–39** *1, 2, 3, 4* D: Tom Stuart-Smith, GB, The Leaf Lounger by Dedon, DE **40–41** *1, 3* The Barn, Herts., GB. D: Tom Stuart-Smith, GB; *2* D: John Morley, GB; *4* Rousham House, GB. D: William Kent, GB; *5* D: George Carter, GB **42–43** *1, 3* Silverstone Farm, GB. D: George Carter, GB; *2* D: André Van Wassenhove, BE **44–45** *1* D: Christopher Bradley-Hole, GB; *2* Landgoed de Wiersse, NL; *3* D: Declan Buckley Design Associates, GB; *4* D: George Carter, GB; *5* D: Tom Stuart-Smith, GB **46–47** Norney Wood, GB. D: Acres Wild Landscape & Garden Design, GB **48–49** *1, 2, 3* Gravetye Manor, GB. D: Tom Coward, GB **50–51** *1, 2, 3* The Manor House, Ayot St Lawrence, GB. D: Julie Toll Landscape & Garden Design, GB, Jacqueline Duncan, GB, gate by ArcAngel Metalworks, GB **52–53** *2* Villa Noailles, Grasse, FR; *3* D: Sue Roscoe-Watts, GB **54–55** *1* D: Alithea Johns, Skopos Design, Corfu, GR; *2* Ashe Park, GB. D: Laura Hazell, GB, Andrew Woolley, GB; *3* D: Shades of Green Landscape Architecture, US; *4* Villa Noailles, Grasse, FR; *5* D: Alyson Deleglise, GR **56–57** *1* D: Kathy Fries, US; *2* D: Sam Martin Exterior Architecture, GB; *3* Pure Land Japanese Garden, GB. D: Buddha Maitreya, GB; *4* D: Acres Wild Landscape & Garden Design, GB; *5* Bloedel Reserve, US. D: Fujitaro Kubota, US **58–59** *1, 2, 3* D: Amir Schlezinger, MyLandscapes, GB **60–61** *1* D: Shades of Green Landscape Architecture, US, Butler Armsden Architects, US, architect: Butler Armsden Architects, US; *2* D: Sue Scrivens, GB; *3* Beth Chatto Gardens, GB; *4* D: Dominick Murphy, Murphy+Sheanon Landscape Architecture, IE **62–63** *1, 2, 3, 4, 5, 6* D: Jenny and Scott Fleming, US **64–65** *1, 2, 3, 4, 5* D: Dominick Murphy, Murphy+Sheanon Landscape Architecture, IE **66–67** D: Susanne Blair Landscape & Garden Design, GB **68–69** *1* D: Tom Stuart-Smith, GB; *2* D: Jamie Dunstan, GB; *3* D: Nan Sinton, US; *4* D: Rosie and Robin Lloyd, GB **70–71** *1* D: Charlotte Rowe Garden Design, GB; *2* De Heerenhof, NL. D: Jan van Opstal and Jo Willems, NL; *3* The Manor House, Ayot St Lawrence, GB. D: John Brookes and Julie Toll, GB; *4* D: Rachel James, GB; *5* D: Rosemary Lindsay, GB **72–75** *1* D: del Buono Gazerwitz Landscape Architecture, GB; *2* D: Mike Harvey, GB; *3* D: Lynne Marcus Garden Design, GB; *4* D: Robert Myers Associates, GB; *5* D: Sara Jane Rothwell, London Garden Designer, GB; *6* D: HTA Design, GB, Noel Kingsbury, GB; *7* Bloedel Reserve, US; *8, 14* June Blake's Garden, IE. D: June Blake, IE; *9* Great Dixter, GB. D: Christopher Lloyd, GB, Fergus Garrett, GB; D: *10* Laara Copley-Smith, GB; *11, 15* Chaumont International Garden Festival, FR; *12* Pinsla, GB; *13* D: Tom Stuart-Smith, GB; *15* D: Hafsa Devauvre and Sacha Goutnova, FR **76–77** *1* D: Carolyn Dunster, Simply Roses, GB; *2* D: Wilson McWilliam Studio, GB; *3* D: Penny Patton, GB **78–81** *1, 3* D: Modular, GB; *2* D: Adele Ford and Susan Willmott, GB; *4* D: Annie Pearce, GB; *5* D: Emma Griffin Garden Design, GB; *6* D: Declan Buckley Design Associates, GB, Dan Cooper, GB; *7* D: Charlotte Rowe Garden Design, GB **82–83** *1* D: Sara Jane Rothwell, London Garden Designer, GB; *2* D: Dominick Murphy, Murphy+Sheanon Landscape Architecture, IE; *3* D: Acres Wild Landscape & Garden Design, GB; *4* Bryan's Ground, GB. D: Simon Dorrell and David Wheeler,

GB **84–85** *1* D: Amber Goudy, GB; *2* D: Amir Schlezinger, MyLandscapes, GB; *3* D: Rupert Wheeler and Paul Gazerwitz, GB; *4* D: Julie Toll Landscape & Garden Design, GB **86–87** *1, 2* D: Lucy Sommers Gardens, GB; *3* D: Jeff and Emma Follas, GB; *4, 5* De Heerenhof, NL. D: Jan van Opstal and Jo Willems, NL **88–89** *1* D: Jane Brockbank Gardens, GB, David Mikhail Architects, GB; *2* D: Gill Richardson, GB; *3* D: Sarah Price Landscapes, GB; *4* D: Chris Ghyselen, BE; *5* D: Julie Toll Landscape & Garden Design, GB; *7* D: Acres Wild Landscape & Garden Design, GB **90–91** *1* The High Line, NY, US. D: James Corner (Field Operations), Diller Scofidio + Renfro, Piet Oudolf, NL; *2* D: Arterra Landscape Architects, US; *3* D: Amir Schlezinger, MyLandscapes, GB; *4* D: Shades of Green Landscape Architecture, US **92–93** *1* D: Shades of Green Landscape Architecture, US; *2* D: Nigel Dunnett, GB; *3* D: Michel Bras, Eric Raffy, Philippe Villeroux, FR; *4* D: Acres Wild Landscape & Garden Design, GB; *5* D: Michèle Osborne, GB; *6* D: Lucy Sommers Gardens, GB; *7* June Blake's Garden, IE. D: June Blake, IE; *8* D: Shades of Green Landscape Architecture, US **94–95** *1* D: Chris Ghyselen, BE; *2* D: Sara Jane Rothwell, London Garden Designer, GB; *3* D: Kathy Fries, US; *4* D: Annie Pearce, GB **96–97** *1* Chygurno, GB; *2* D: Rosemary Alexander, GB; *3* D: Charlotte Rowe Garden Design, GB; *4* D: Sue Townsend Garden Design, GB **98–99** *1, 4, 5, 8* D: Julie Toll Landscape & Garden Design, GB; *2* D: DesignWild Associates, GB; *3* D: Peter Berg, GartenLandschaft Berg, DE; *6* June Blake's Garden, IE. D: June Blake, IE; *7* D: Acres Wild Landscape & Garden Design, GB **100–101** *1* D: Sara Jane Rothwell, London Garden Designer, GB; *2* D: Anthony Paul Landscape Design, GB; *3* D: Charlotte Rowe Garden Design, GB; *4* D: Stuart Craine Design, GB; *5* D: Christopher Bradley-Hole, GB; *6* D: Todd Longstaffe-Gowan, GB; *7* D: Malcolm Hillier, GB **102–103** *1* D: Modular, GB; *2* D: Wilson McWilliam Studio, GB; *3* D: Jane Brockbank Gardens, GB, David Mikhail Architects, GB **104–105** *1* The Manor House, Ayot St Lawrence, GB. D: Julie Toll Landscape & Garden Design, GB, ArcAngel Metalworks, GB; *2* D: Sara Jane Rothwell, London Garden Designer, GB; *3* Feeringbury Manor, GB; *4* D: Wirtz International Landscape Architects, BE **106–107** *1* www.naturalfencing.com; *2* Danecroft, GB; *3* Sea Gem, Camber Sands, GB. D: Jo Thompson Landscape & Garden Design, GB **108–109** *1* London Wetland Centre, GB. D: Cleve West and Johnny Woodford, GB; *2* D: Sally Brampton, GB; *4* D: Wendy Smith and Fern Alder, GB **110–111** *1* D: Charlotte Rowe Garden Design, GB; *2* D: Liz Robinson, GB; *3, 4* D: Sara Jane Rothwell, London Garden Designer, GB; *5* D: Christopher Bradley-Hole, GB; *6* D: Annie Pearce, GB **112–113** *1* Sezincote, GB; *2* D: Alison Sloga, GB; *3* D: Christopher Bradley-Hole, GB **114–117** *1* D: Julie Toll Landscape & Garden Design, GB; *3* D: Annie Pearce, GB; *4* D: Sue Townsend Garden Design, GB; *5* D: Stuart Craine Design, GB; *6* D: Arterra Landscape Architects, US; *7* D: François Valentiny, HVP Architects, LU; *8* D: Wirtz International Landscape Architects, BE; *9* D: Shades of Green Landscape Architecture, US **118–121** *1* D: Jenny Raworth, GB; *2* Anglesey Abbey, GB; *3* D: Chris Ghyselen, BE; *4* D: del Buono Gazerwitz Landscape Architecture, GB, loop chair by Willy Guhl, CH; *5* D: Paul Southern, P.S.Gardens, GB; *6* Cothay Manor, GB; *7* Elton Hall, GB; *8* Penshurst Place, GB **122–123** *1* D: Tom Stuart-Smith, GB, Jamie Fobert Architects, GB; *2* D: Theresa-Mary Morton, GB; *3* Wollerton Old Hall, GB; *4* D: George Carter, GB; *6* Shandy Hall, GB; *7* D: Sue Roscoe-Watts, GB; *8* Landgoed de Wiersse, NL. De Wiersse, NL **124–125** *2* D: Heather Appleton, GB; *3* D: del Buono Gazerwitz Landscape Architecture, GB, bowl and chairs by Faye Toogood, GB; *4* D: Ana Sanchez-Martin, Germinate Design, GB **126–127** *1* D: Marion Jay, GB; *2* D: Kathy Fries, US; *3* June Blake's Garden, IE. D: June Blake, IE; *4* Sandhill Farm House, GB. D: Rosemary Alexander, GB; *5* Furzelea, GB. D: Avril and Roger Cole-Jones; *6* D: Andy Sturgeon Landscape and Garden Design, GB; *7* D: Christopher Masson, GB **128–129** *1* Helmingham Hall, GB. D: Xa Tollemache, GB; *2* West Dean Gardens, GB. D: Sarah Wain and Jim Buckland, GB; *3* D: Caroline Holmes, GB; *4* Bedfield Hall, GB. D: Timothy and Christine Easton; *5* Barnsley House, GB. D: Rosemary Verey, GB **130–131** *1* The Garden of Cosmic Speculation, GB. D: Charles Jencks, GB; *2, 5* D: Christopher Bradley-Hole, GB; *3* Dartington Hall, GB; *4* St Michael's Mount, GB **132–133** *1* D: Alison Wear, GB; *2* The Garden of Cosmic Speculation, GB. D: Charles Jencks, GB; *3* Marks Hall, GB. D: Brita von Schoenaich Landscape Architects, GB **134–135** *1* D: Rita Streitz, LU; *3* D: Peter Berg, GartenLandschaft Berg, DE; *4* D: Modular, GB **136–137** *2* D: Shades of Green Landscape Architecture, US; *3* D: Claire Mee Garden Design, GB; *4* The Olympic Park, London, GB. D: LDA and Nigel Dunnett, GB **138–139** D: Emma Griffin Garden Design, GB **140–141** *3* D: Hugh Johnson, GB; *6* D: Christopher Bradley-Hole, GB **142–143** *1* Hermannshof, DE. D: Cassian Schmidt, DE; *2* D: Jill Billington, GB; *3* D: Nan Sinton, US; *4* Westonbirt Arboretum, GB; *5* D: Chris Ghyselen, BE; *6* D: Arterra Landscape Architects, US **144–147** *1* The Old Vicarage, East Ruston, GB. D: Alan Gray and Graham Robeson, GB; *10* The High Line, NY, US. D: James Corner (Field Operations), Diller Scofidio + Renfro, Piet Oudolf, NL; *11* Anglesey Abbey, GB; *12* Glen Chantry, GB. D: Sue and Wol Staines, GB **148–149** *1* Tuin 't Hofje, NL. D: Joke Cijsouw, NL; *3* Filoli, US **150–153** *1* D: del Buono Gazerwitz Landscape Architecture, GB; *2, 3* D: Christopher

Bradley-Hole, GB; *4* D: Julie Toll Landscape & Garden Design, GB; *5* D: Dominick Murphy, Murphy+Sheanon Landscape Architecture, IE; *6* Barnsley House, GB. D: Rosemary Verey, GB; *7* D: Sue Townsend Garden Design, GB; *8* Green Island Gardens, GB. D: Fiona Edmond, GB **154–155** *2* D: René Meyers, LU; *4* D: Amédée Turner, GB, Friday Harper, GB; *5* D: Amir Schlezinger, MyLandscapes, GB **156–157** *1* D: Ric Ide, US; *2* D: Brian and Dawn Dunn, GB; *3* D: George Cameron Nash, US **158–159** *1* D: René Meyers, LU; *2* Insel Mainau, DE; *4* Tuin 't Hofje, NL. D: Joke Cijsouw, NL **160–161** *2* D: Nico Hoffmann, LU; *3* D: Christopher Bradley-Hole, GB; *4* West Green House, GB. D: Marylyn Abbott, GB; *5* D: John Brookes, GB; *6* D: Judith Sharpe Garden Design, GB **162–163** *1, 2, 3* D: André Van Wassenhove, BE **164–165** *1* D: del Buono Gazerwitz Landscape Architecture, GB; *3* De Heerenhof, NL. D: Jan van Opstal and Jo Willems, NL; *4* D: François Valentiny, HVP Architects, LU; *5* D: Marc Schoellen, LU **166–167** *1* D: Rita Streitz, LU; *2* D: Christopher Bradley-Hole, GB; *3* D: Penelope Hobhouse, GB; *4* D: Annette Block and Claude Vion, LU **168–171** *3* D: Tigger Cullinan, GB; *6* Bramdean House, GB. D: Victoria Wakefield, GB **172–173** *1* RHS Garden, Wisley; *2* D: Carine Reckinger-Thrill, LU **174–175** *1* Greenway, GB; *4* D: Sue Martin, GB **176–177** *3* Boconnoc, GB; *4* Ramster, GB **180–181** *1* D: Carine Reckinger-Thrill, LU; *2* D: Claire Mee Designs, GB; *3* D: Emile Becker, LU; *4* The Dunn Garden, WA, US **182–183** *1, 2, 3* D: Emile Becker, LU **184–185** *1* The Elisabeth Carey Miller Botanical Garden, WA, US; *3* Chestnut Farm, GB; *4* The Old Vicarage, East Ruston. D: Alan Gray and Graham Robeson, GB; *5* The Garden House, GB **186–187** *1* Haddon Lake House, GB. D: Phillippa Lambert, GB; *2* Wollerton Old Hall, GB. D: John and Lesley Jenkins, GB; *3* D: Nori and Sandra Pope, GB **188–189** *1* Hunting Brook Gardens, IE. D: Jimi Blake, IE; *2* Sleightholmedale Lodge, GB. D: Rosanna James, GB; *3* Glen Chantry, GB. D: Sue and Wol Staines, GB; *5* The Dunn Garden, WA, US **190–191** *1* D: Christopher Bradley-Hole, GB; *2* D: Stuart Craine Design, GB, Dyer Grimes Architects, GB; *4* D: Julie Toll Landscape & Garden Design, GB **192–195** *1* D: Christopher Bradley-Hole, GB; *2* D: Tom Stuart-Smith, GB; *3* D: Philip Nixon Design, GB; *4* D: André Van Wassenhove, BE; *5* D: Nan Sinton, US; *6* Ashe Park, GB; *7* Greenway, GB; *8* Woodpeckers, GB. D: Andy and Lallie Cox, GB **196–197** *2, 3* D: Jane Brockbank Gardens, GB; *5* The Old Vicarage, East Ruston, GB. D: Alan Gray and Graham Robeson, GB **218–219** *1, 2, 3* D: René Meyers, LU **220–221** *1, 2, 3, 4* Dove Cottage, GB. D: Stephen and Kim Rogers, GB **222–223** *1* D: Chris Ghyselen, BE; *2* D: Christopher Bradley-Hole, GB; *3* Sussex Prairies, GB. D: Paul and Pauline McBride, GB; *4* Dove Cottage, GB. D: Stephen and Kim Rogers, GB **224–225** *1, 2, 3* Sussex Prairies, GB. D: Paul and Pauline McBride, GB **226–229** *1* Manor Farm, GB. D: Gill Richardson, GB; *2, 4* Hunting Brook Gardens, IE. D: Jimi Blake, IE; *3* Dove Cottage, GB. D: Stephen and Kim Rogers, GB; *5* The Dillon Garden, IE. D: Helen Dillon, IE; *6* June Blake's Garden, IE. D: June Blake, IE; *7* D: Christopher Bradley-Hole, GB; *8* Great Dixter, GB. D: Christopher Lloyd, GB, Fergus Garrett, GB **230–231** The Barn, Herts., GB. D: Tom Stuart-Smith, GB **232–233** *1, 2, 3, 4* D: Declan Buckley Design Associates, GB **234–235** *1* D: Gay Edwards, GB; *2* De Heerenhof, NL. D: Jan van Opstal and Jo Willems, NL; *3* D: Claire Mee Designs, GB; *5* D: Hetty van Baalen, NL **236–237** *1, 2, 3, 4* Ulting Wick, GB. D: Philippa Burrough, GB **238–239** *1* Marchants Hardy Plants, GB. D: Graham Gough, GB; *2* Beth Chatto Gardens, GB; *3* D: Sue Townsend Garden Design, GB; *4* Great Dixter, GB. D: Christopher Lloyd, GB, Fergus Garrett, GB **240–243** *1* D: John Bailey, The Soho Gardener, GB; *2* D: Marty Hoffmann, LU; *4* Haddon Lake House, GB. D: Phillippa Lambert, GB; *5* D: Paul and Patsy Harrington, GB; *6* D: John Bailey, The Soho Gardener, GB; *7* D: Charles Roovers and Dieter Lingener, LU; *8, 9* Lamorran House Gardens, GB; *10* Henstead Exotic Garden, GB. D: Andrew Brogan, The Real Garden Company, GB **244–245** *1* Clergy House, GB; *2* Bunny Guinness, GB; *4* Haddon Lake House, GB. D: Phillippa Lambert, GB **246–247** *1* Gravetye Manor, GB. D: Tom Coward, GB; *2* Scampston Hall, GB; *4* Rosemary Verey, GB **248–249** *1, 2* Barnsley House, GB. D: Rosemary Verey, GB; *3* The Barn, Herts., GB. D: Tom Stuart-Smith, GB **250–251** *1, 2, 3* Ashe Park, GB. *4* Scampston Hall. D: Laura Hazell, GB, Andrew Woolley, GB **252–255** *1* D: Bunny Guinness, GB; *2* D: Patricia Fox, Aralia Garden

Design, GB; *3* West Green House, GB. D: Marylyn Abbott, GB; *4* Gunnebo House, SE. D: Joakim Seiler, SE; *6, 8* D: Claire Mee Designs, GB; *7* D: George Carter, GB **256–257** *1, 2, 3, 4* D: Emma Griffin Garden Design, GB, Sarah Wigglesworth Architects, GB **258–259** West Green House, GB. D: Marylyn Abbott, GB **260–261** *1* D: Carine Reckinger-Thrill, LU; *2* The Barn, Herts., GB. D: Tom Stuart-Smith, GB; *3* D: Spencer Viner, North Eleven Garden Design, GB; *4* D: Lucy Sommers Gardens, GB; *5* D: Stuart Craine Design, GB, Dyer Grimes Architects, GB; *6* Sandringham House, GB **262–263** *1* West Green House, GB. D: Marylyn Abbott, GB; *2* D: Stuart Craine Design, GB; *3* Endsleigh House, GB. D: Humphry Repton; *4* Rousham House, GB. D: William Kent, GB; *5* The Connaught Hotel, London, GB. D: Tom Stuart-Smith, GB; *6* D: Anthony Paul Landscape Design, GB; *7, 8* Banque Générale du Luxembourg, LU. D: Wirtz International Landscape Architects, BE **264–265** *1* Les jardins d'Annevoie, BE; *2* D: Piet Oudolf, NL, and Arne Maynard, GB; *3* D: Olivia Kirk Gardens, GB; *4* D: Acres Wild Landscape & Garden Design, GB; *5* D: Amir Schlezinger, MyLandscapes, GB; *6* D: Catherine Heatherington Designs, GB; *7* Insel Mainau, DE; *8* Hampton Court, Hre., GB. D: Simon Dorrell, GB **266–267** *1* D: Tom Stuart-Smith, GB; *2* Brightling Down Farm, GB. D: Acres Wild Landscape & Garden Design, GB; *3* Uggeshall Hall, GB. D: Stevie Nicholson, GB; *4* Julie Toll Landscape & Garden Design, GB; *5* D: Paolo Pejrone, IT **268–269** *1* Scampston Hall, GB. D: Piet Oudolf, NL; *2* D: Carine Reckinger-Thrill, LU; *3* Flora Grubb Gardens, US; *4* Sea Gem, Camber Sands, GB; *5* D: Lynne Marcus Garden Design, GB; *6* Hunting Brook Gardens, IE. D: Jimi Blake, IE **270–271** *1* Sussex Prairies, GB. D: Paul and Pauline McBride, GB; *2* Seat D: Alison Crowther, GB; *3* D: George Carter, GB; *4* Bench D: Will Sandy Landscape Architecture and Design, GB; *5* D: Sydvast arkitektur och landskap, SE; *6* D: Charlotte Rowe Garden Design, GB; *7* Bench by Jim Partridge and Liz Walmsley, GB; *8* D: Sue Townsend Garden Design, GB, bench by Marnie Moyle, GB, bench by Marnie Moyle, GB; *9* D: Anthony Paul Landscape Design, GB; *10* Bench D: Ben Barrell, GB **272–273** *1* D: Claire Mee Designs, GB; *2* D: Spencer Viner, North Eleven Garden Design, GB; *3* D: Lloyd Birchmore and Terry Clare, GB; *4* D: Anthony Paul Landscape Design, GB; *5* D: Marion Jay, GB; *6* D: François Valentiny, HVP Architects, LU; *7* D: Catherine Heatherington Designs, GB **274–277** *1* D: Tom Stuart-Smith, GB, Jamie Fobert Architects, GB; *2, 6* D: Lynne Marcus Garden Design, GB; *3* The Old Rectory, Farnborough, GB; *4* D: Jamie Fobert Architects, GB; *5* D: del Buono Gazerwitz Landscape Architecture, GB, Charles Barclay Architects, GB, architect: Charles Barclay, GB; *7* Henstead Exotic Garden, GB. D: Andrew Brogan, GB, The Real Garden Company, GB; *9* Lowder Mill, GB. D: Anne and John Denning, GB; *10* Zaki and Ruth Elia, GB; *11* Manor Farm, Thixendale, GB. D: Gilda Brader, GB **278–279** *1, 3* D: Charlotte Rowe Garden Design, GB; *2* D: Lucy Sommers Gardens, GB; *4* D: Amir Schlezinger, MyLandscapes, GB; *5* D: Claire Mee Designs, GB **280–281** *1* D: Paul Cooper, GB; *2* D: Adam Shepherd, The Landscape Architect, GB; *3* Henstead Exotic Garden, GB. D: Andrew Brogan, GB, The Real Garden Company, GB **282–287** *1* Sussex Prairies, GB. Flying Saucers' by Robin Johnson, GB; *2* A flock of seagulls' by Jack Trowbridge, GB, Mazey Cottage, GB. D: Marion Stanley, 'A flock of seagulls' by Jack Trowbridge, GB; *3* D: Christopher Bradley-Hole, GB, sculpture by Ron Arad, GB; *4* Sussex Prairies, GB. D: Paul and Pauline McBride, GB; *5* Sussex Prairies, GB. Hollopod oak sculpture by Si Uwins, GB; *6* Lead seedpod sculpture by Jim Whitson, GB; *7* Denmans, GB. Bird sculptures by Marion Smith, GB; *8* Pinsla Garden, GB. D: Mark and Claire Woodbine, GB; *9* Presence' by Michael Speller, GB, garden D: Lynne Marcus Garden Design, GB, 'Presence' by Michael Speller, GB; *10* Walnuts by Landscape Ornament Company, GB; *11* Sculpture by Josiane Marschal, LU; *12* Sculpture by Bruno Romeda, FR; *13* D: Gordon McArthur and Paul Thompson, GB; *14* Sculpture by Nancy Train Smith, US; *15* D: Roger Platts Garden Design, GB; *16* D: Reginald Neuman, sculpture by Marta Pan, HU **288–289** D: Adam Shepherd, The Landscape Architect, GB **290–291** *1, 5* Amir Schlezinger, MyLandscapes, GB; *2* D: Sam Martin Exterior Architecture, GB, and Richard Holden Architects, GB; *3* D: Fiona Naylor, GB; *4* D: Lynne Marcus Garden Design, GB **292–293** *1* D: Amir Schlezinger, MyLandscapes, GB; *2* D: Emma Griffin Garden Design, GB, Sarah Wigglesworth Architects, GB; *3* D: Christopher Bradley-Hole, GB; *4* D: Marie Brandolini, IT **294–295** *1* D: Edwina Roberts, GB; *2* D: Arterra Landscape Architects, US; *3* D: Amir Schlezinger, MyLandscapes, GB; *4* D: Helen and James Dooley, SE **296–297** *1* The Dillon Garden, IE. D: Helen Dillon, IE; *2* D: del Buono Gazerwitz Landscape Architecture, GB; *3* D: Amir Schlezinger, MyLandscapes, GB; *4* D: Claire Mee Designs, GB **298–299** *1* D: Shades of Green Landscape Architecture, US; *2* St Michael's Mount, GB; *3* D: HTA Design, GB, Noel Kingsbury, GB; *4* D: Declan Buckley Design Associates, GB **300–301** *1, 2, 6* D: Wendy Booth and Leslie Howell, GB; *3, 5* Chygurno, GB; *4* D: Christopher Holliday, GB **302–303** *1* The Driver, London, GB. D: Patrick Blanc, FR; *2* D: Marie Clarke, Clarke Associates, GB; *3* D: Christopher Masson, GB; *4* D: Fiona Heyes Landscape and Garden Design, GB **304–305** *1* D: George Carter, GB; *2* D: Modular, GB; *3* D: Henrietta Courtauld, GB **306–307** *1, 2, 3, 4, 5* D: Adam Shepherd, The Landscape Architect, GB **308–309** *1* D: Declan Buckley Design Associates, GB; *2, 3* D: del Buono Gazerwitz Landscape Architecture, GB, loop chair by Willy Guhl, CH; *4* D: George Carter, GB **310–311** *1* Wickham Place Farm, GB; *2* Kiftsgate Court Gardens, GB; *3* D: Jessica Duncan, GB **312–313** Gravetye Manor, GB.